How to write
Your First
NOVEL

A Guide For Aspiring Fiction Authors

An Author Your Ambition Book
by M.K. Williams

First printing edition 2021.

ISBN: 978-1-952084-43-0 (Paperback), 978-1-952084-44-7 (Hardcover)

Library of Congress Control Number: 2020922514

Second edition, 2025

Printed by M.K. Williams Publishing, LLC in the United States of America.

authoryourambition@gmail.com

www.authoryourambition.com

Cover Design by 100Covers

HOW TO WRITE YOUR FIRST NOVEL

Works by M.K. Williams

Fiction

The Project Collusion Series

Nailbiters

Architects

The Feminina Series

The Infinite-Infinite

The Alpha-Nina

Other Fiction

The Games You Cannot Win

Escaping Avila Chase

Enemies of Peace

Interview with a #Vanlifer

Non-Fiction

Self-Publishing for the First-Time Author

Book Marketing for the First-Time Author

How to Write Your First Novel: A Guide for Aspiring Fiction Authors

Going Wide: Self-Publishing Your Books Outside The Amazon Ecosystem

Author Your Ambition: The Complete Self-Publishing Workbook for First-Time Authors

Works by Mary Kate Williams

Fiction

Genisse

Contents

Dedication   VI

Introduction   1

Part 1: You Need More Than Just An Idea   6

1. Dedicate Time To Write   8

2. Dedicate Space And Attention To Writing   18

3. Do Your Research   26

4. Goals And Getting It Done   32

Part 2: Elements Of Your Novel   37

5. Voice And Structure - How To Actually Write The Dang   39
   Thing?

6. Plot - Writing That Compels The Reader To Turn The   62
   Page

7. Creating Three-Dimensional Characters   74

8. Bring It All Together   88

9. The Revision Process Begins   96

Conclusion   102

Acknowledgements   104

Dedication

To all the aspiring authors who dream, plan, write, and work hard to make it a reality.

Introduction

My Story

I pulled my gloves off just as the elevator arrived. It was another freezing January evening in Philadelphia. The cold clung to my clothes for a few moments after I entered Creese Hall. Home to the University Bookstore, Administration offices for each department, and the Drexel University Honors College, I headed to one of the few classrooms in the building. It was almost 6 pm, and I was eager to arrive on time for this class.

I'm not sure many 20-year-olds would characterize themselves as excited about attending a 3-hour seminar class at 6 pm on a Monday. But I wasn't most 20-year-olds, and this wasn't just any class.

My Economics major and affinity for math-jokes may have fooled some, but I was a word nerd at my core. When I saw a course called "Writing Killer Fiction" in the winter term catalog, I made sure I was the first to sign up.

I entered the narrow room and took my seat at a long table. In total, there were eight students in the class and one professor. Cordelia Biddle, a published author, made the term assignment easy to understand from that first night. Over the next ten weeks, each of us was to compose a short story. Each week, a different scene would be due for critique, and the final assignment would be to stitch these scenes together into one narrative. She gave us guidance on character, plot, suspense, red-herrings, and all the goodies that readers love.

The assignment was to write a 50-page short story.

Most of my classmates did this with ease. A few began to worry that they wouldn't make the page count.

I didn't finish, though.

As the end of term approached, I knew that my story was nowhere near done. I had 100 pages in a Microsoft Word document, and I knew there was more to the story I still had to write. I told Professor Biddle that I hadn't completed the assignment. She told me to get a membership to a professional writer's association and consider attending conferences. I got an A in the class.

A year later, after I graduated (in the middle of a deep recession), I pulled that story back out and worked on it bit by bit each day until I finished the manuscript.

I had completed my first novel. And I had no idea what to do next.

The most significant advantage that my coursework provided was dedicated time to get the book written. Of the aspiring authors that I meet today, most of them who share their desire to write a book haven't even started. Hands-down, the hardest thing about writing a book is writing it.

Don't get me wrong, finding an audience, maximizing your ranking on Amazon, and dealing with tricky ePub formatting can be a real pain as well. But none of those things matter if you don't get your words written.

Over the years since I wrote my first novel, friends and acquaintances have asked for help getting their own book started. At the outset, my advice was, "you sit at your computer and write." But I realized that their trepidation about writing their novel had nothing to do with the mechanics of turning on a computer, opening a word processor, and typing. Their concerns were about craft, story-telling, suspense, and the creation of art.

As I have tried to articulate an answer to, "how do you write a novel?" I have refined my response. Now, when I work with clients looking for the beginning steps, I break down the book's critical elements. Setting out on this journey to write a novel isn't like starting at the beginning of a trail with a specific route to a mountain's peak. There are multiple points where you can begin and elements that you'll want to include. But no defined path that everyone must follow.

I will provide you with guidance on those necessary items, and a few of the optional ones as well, so that you can write your first novel.

The Story Never Ends

When I wrote this guide in 2021, I really thought I knew what I was doing. I had a solid routine for writing and editing my books. My audience was growing. Book sales were charting up and up.

For the most part, my process hasn't changed too much. I have less time to write now that I have a daughter to care for. But I wouldn't trade the time with her for anything.

I outline more now than I used to. I've found that with less time (to think, to write, to focus on my career) I can't wait for the story to find me. But I also get impatient and just want to write the dang thing.

Another factor I didn't address in the first edition is Artificial Intelligence. At the time, A.I. was already upon us, but not nearly as pervasive and easily accessible as it is now. At least once a month someone asks me how my writing is going and then follows it up with a question about A.I. Because the headlines make it seem as though all books will now be written by A.I. and humans will never be free to express themselves creatively again.

Hmm, how many A.I. written books are on the bestseller lists? How long can they stay there once the reviews come in?

I don't use A.I. in the creation of my books. Not for idea generation. Not for plotting. Not for any of it. I enjoy the creative process, I'm not about to outsource it. Especially not to the systems that scraped a pirated copy of my book to train their Large Language Model (LLM).

That is to say, if you're looking for a guide to tell you how to use A.I. to write a book: this isn't the guide for you. This guide is for people with so many creative ideas they don't know where to get started. Plagiarists masquerading as "A.I. enthusiasts" need not continue any further.

Maxims, Truisms, The Advice You've Already Heard

As a writer, we often lament that all of our good ideas must have already been written. All the brilliant things have been said. Maybe that is true for some topics, but it is absolutely not true for writing. Still, how can I say something more clever than Hemingway, more profound than Austen? Who am I to try and put a new spin on their words?

You can log onto your social media right now and find memorable quotes by prolific authors by searching #authorquotes. They will look very stylish, and they will inspire you, but then what?

I'm not here to regurgitate what others have said. I'm here to tell you what I have done and what has worked for me. I do that to help you reach your goal.

Yes, you should write what you know. But you know more than what you've studied in school. You know your life experience. You know what you've felt. Yes, you do need to spend time in the chair. We'll get to that later.

Yes, you should write every day because not everything you write will be great or even good. You need to get the bad writing out. And you do that by practicing every day. You can't go weeks or even months without writing and expect to write the next great American novel. Just like a pianist can't go weeks or months without practicing and plan to put on a performance worthy of a major stage.

Nothing that I will tell you here is earth-shattering or brand new, but I hope that the way I explain it will propel you towards your goal. I've followed the advice of the great authors who came before me. What I will tell you are my specific tactics and strategies that have helped me and the multitude of authors I have worked with. My aim here is to inspire you, yes. But most importantly, I want to give you actionable tips that you apply today to get your book written.

I will help break down the different steps that have been critical to my success in writing multiple novels. This book is not a strict how-to regimen that you need to follow. It is the best of what I have learned by trial and error. I'll review both the act of actually writing and how to get the words down, and also the craft that goes into making those words a story.

What follows is my process for writing a novel. I hope this helps you on your journey and that you will soon be able to write "THE END" in your own manuscript.

Part 1: You Need More Than Just An Idea

So many people have an idea for a story. They see something during the course of their day and think, "huh, that would make an interesting book." Or they believe their life is fit for retelling in print. Ideas are out there, like molecules of oxygen. Ideas are everywhere.

Your idea is going to be the next best-selling book turned blockbuster. Your idea is going to inspire millions. Your idea is going to launch you from a part-time author to full Stephen King status.

But the idea in and of itself can't do anything. It sits in your mind until you take action. It's a single-celled organism. It can't grow into anything useful until it latches onto a host. Just because this idea is in your mind doesn't mean it will become a book.

When you start putting pen to paper, the idea grows arms and hands and fingers. When you type it onto a blank page, it develops legs and fine motor skills.

Your idea needs you to write and expand on the original concept to make it into something.

When I interact with aspiring authors, there is never a shortage of ideas that inspire them. But most of them haven't written a word. One reason is the lack of focus and commitment. You need more than just a bunch of ideas; you need to write them down. (*Thanks, Captain Obvious! You're Welcome!*)

I didn't set out to write this guide to state the obvious. So how do ideas turn into a full-fledged novel? First, you need to dedicate time, space, and focus on getting the words out. What we'll review first are the different aspects to completing this task.

Chapter One

Dedicate Time To Write

S aturday afternoons were sacred for my writing practice. And this is because of football.

Yes, you read that right. Football. My husband and I both enjoy the sport and while we are polite people with perfect manners, just wait for a Philadelphia Eagles game to hear my extended vocabulary. I grew up rooting for the Eagles and followed professional football. My husband favors college ball. He roots for his alma mater, The University of South Florida Bulls, and watches each of their games. He also likes to watch all of the other Florida teams. Saturdays are very busy for him. In contrast, I don't feel the need to pay attention until I see the Eagles kickoff on Sundays.

Do you see where I am going with this? Saturdays are my special days to write and write and write. My husband and I can sit next to each other on the couch and chit chat when I get to a spot where I need to pause, but otherwise, I get to write. This was our harmonious pattern as I tried to write my novels while still overachieving at my day job. (He may have thought he would get my attention on those games once I became a full-time author, but Saturdays are still great writing days.)

The reason that I tell you this is that you don't have to buy into the antiquated image of the reclusive writer who ignores their family and friends, who sacrifices it all to get their story written. That is ridiculous. You don't get a medal for finishing your book while ignoring everything else in your life. The real prize is finishing your novel and getting to share it with those who supported you along the way. That doesn't mean there won't be any sacrifices though. It is a delicate balance.

Here are the top things that I have done to make sure my manuscripts progress into finished books:

Set Priorities

I have never seen a single episode of Game of Thrones. I don't rush out to watch the latest movie when it hits the theater. I don't binge the new hot series when it drops.

You may think I am a reclusive weirdo who is out of touch. But I know that I am prioritizing my time. My goals involve writing books and helping others publish their books as well. Those are time-intensive tasks. I can't spend hours each day watching content that isn't moving me closer to my goals. The priority that I have set is on content creation, not consumption.

For me, watching TV is easy to cut. But that may not be the same for you.

In order to set your priorities in terms of what will get done, you need to first look at how you are currently spending your time. This is a quick and easy time audit. Are you surfing the web while you are at work, meaning that you have to work a little later to keep up? Can you cut out those web-breaks so that you can get home at a better hour and get some writing in? Can you prepare lunch ahead of time and use 30-minutes of that time for dedicated writing?

How about social media? Can you put your phone in another room for one hour to make sure you are focused on getting your writing in? I installed the QualityTime app on my phone to see how much time I spent checking my social media. I was shocked! I thought I was so good at not wasting time. It turns out I'm human. So, I put the phone in another room.

And then, I took it to the next level. My husband and I instituted a rule for 90 days; if either of us wanted to check our social media, we had to ask the other person. Even if we were at work. It sounds weird, but it helped us to make better decisions with our time. If I sent him a text about my stressful workload, I couldn't ask to waste time on Facebook a few minutes later. When we were sitting at the dinner table each night, we had actual conversations with each other.

Because who was going to be the jerk and ask to scroll their feed when we had a freshly cooked meal in front of us? This technique worked for us, and it kept me from wasting time when I should have been writing my book. It helped me to keep my priorities in order.

You don't need to go to these extremes, though. You can set your phone face-down on your desk or table. That can be a simple reminder that it is time to write. If it is really tempting, you can add a post-it note to the back that reads "Phone Down, Word Count Up." You'll find a little reminder or process that works for you, but the main point here is to cut out the time-wasters.

Next, write down your five biggest priorities in your life right now. For me, my priorities are:

1. My health - I make time every day to work out and prepare healthy meals. If I'm not healthy, then I can't show up for any of my other priorities.

2. My relationships with my husband and child- Without my partner and baby to share it all with, I would have nothing.

3. My family - I have lost loved ones, and I never want to regret having missed time with them.

4. My writing - I love to write; it inspires and gives me joy.

5. My friends - They keep me grounded and smiling.

If I spend time doing something that doesn't align with those priorities, I usually stop doing that thing. I would encourage you to do the same. Is a friend of a friend of a friend guilting you into organizing an event for them? Unless that person is a priority in your life, you can say no. Is that plotline in a TV show a bigger priority than quality time with your family? Are those social updates more important than completing your book?

The good news about priorities is that they change over time. Once you write your book, you may decide that your writing time can move down the priority list for the next season of your life. And, you can reward your hard work and catch up or binge your favorite show after you finish your book. You'll find the right balance.

Find The Time To Write

The time that you need to write your book is there. It is in the moments that you spend delaying getting off the couch. It is in the time you take to make mundane decisions over what to wear or eat for lunch. Even as I write this book, I am waiting for a conference call to start. It was supposed to begin ten minutes ago. I figured this might happen, that the caller might be delayed, so I had my document open, just in case. And now, I'm getting words written instead of lamenting the wasted time.

We only waste as much time as we allow ourselves. Our time is allocated, all of it. So much for sleeping, commuting, working. Every day that we stay a little late at work to clean out emails, we choose to spend our time that way. Each day that we use our lunch hour to scroll social media or gossip with coworkers, we decide to spend time on those activities.

Yes, dedicating every spare second to writing your book is a commitment. It is a challenge. If writing your book were easy, you would have done it by now. As someone who did this for years, I can guarantee you that the TV shows will be recorded for you when your book is finished. The office politics will likely be in just the same state six months from now. You may be sacrificing time with friends, but refer back to your priority list. When you are with your friends and family, are you committed to giving them your time and attention? If yes, then you know you can count on their support and respecting your goal of writing this book. If no, then recommit to being focused when you are with them. Then you can say without reservation that you have given them quality time and now you need to get back to your book.

There is something to be said for balance. For silence. For moments when you can relax and turn your brain off. When you can meditate. But for me, as I suppose this applies to you too, if I don't get the words out, I can't relax. I need to put them onto paper so I can clear my mind.

Writing Challenges And Communities

I can't go too much further without stopping to discuss writing challenges and communities to help you prioritize and find time to write. Back when I was starting the draft of my very first novel, I had a specific word count I had to reach every week. That was the homework for our writing seminar. I had to have a new chapter done to present to the group.

While you may not take an official course in creative writing with its built-in deadlines, you can set one for yourself. This can be as simple as setting a goal to write an average of 1,000 words a day. If you hit the average at the end of the week, you can treat yourself to a special dessert or another gift. Because we live in an age of social media, you can share your progress with your network. This can provide some great accountability and help you connect with other authors who are doing the same.

A quick search on your social media platform of choice will reveal threads on word counts and writing sprints. You can probably find a group to join that will encourage your writing goals. Some focus around a specific word count per day, while others are support groups where authors can share their daily word counts and encourage each other to push for more. Occasionally, you may join a writing live-stream on Facebook or YouTube. This is where one writer will broadcast from their desk as they are writing, and others can join in to write with them. Think of it as a virtual writing circle. I haven't joined in on these, but I know many authors who do.

Perhaps the most well-known writing challenge was NaNoWriMo. This stands for National Novel Writing Month, which is usually every November. The aim is to write 50,000 words in 30 days. Many authors prepare for this event all year, trying to get their story development work done ahead of the challenge.

In recent years, the NaNoWriMo challenge has made statements encouraging the use of A.I. in plotting and drafting, while partnering with an A.I. company. Maybe this turns you off from participating in their challenge. There are other similar ones hosted that you can join. In April 2025, the non-profit announced it was going to close.

While this hosted challenge and the website tracking may not exist anymore, you can set up your own challenge. This can be a monthly or even a daily task. I find that if I have a printed tracker sheet with the date across the top and my goal for each day down the side that I will be more likely to hit my daily goal. Being able to check off or color in the daily goal tracker helps me to stay motivated and it is a fun challenge, even if I don't share it with anyone. But, for those of you who know you need a challenge and accountability, tell the world what you are trying to do! People want to see you succeed so post your daily, weekly, or monthly wordcount goal online and let those regular posts serve as your accountability check in. You'll be surprised how many friends ask you how your writing is going, which means you better have something good to tell them.

You'll find the right system that works for you. For your first novel, write what you can when you can. Opting in or creating your own word count challenge could help you reach your goal that much sooner. Having the support of an author community can also make the very solitary process a little less lonely.

Inspiration Will Strike

While you have carved out a dedicated time to write, you may find that the creative part of your brain does not want to comply. You may sit down to your computer and draw a total blank. *What was I trying to say when I left off here? Who are these characters that I invented?*

Conversely, you may get all of your unique ideas just as you are dozing off to sleep. This happens to me. I will occasionally wake up from a dream with a very vivid and clear vision for a scene in a book or some perfect dialogue. My designated writing time is not right before bed, or the second I wake up.

These ideas are fleeting. They only exist in small corners of our minds, and we need to write them down.

How do we get the ideas down and still honor our designated writing time? My solution is a good ole-fashioned notebook. I found some spiral-bound notebooks at our local pharmacy a few years ago. They are roughly 2"x3" and have a colorful thin plastic cover. I think I spent a little over a dollar after tax for each of these. As a writer, I am often gifted notebooks as well. These notebooks are your best friend. You can write down an idea and come back to it later during your writing time.

Sometimes I have to get the idea down quickly, and when I go back to read it, I struggle with some of the words. (I have horrible penmanship). But, I still get the jist. Many people will say that you have to go to your word processor the instant inspiration strikes. Well, if you are in the middle of your corporate workday, that may not be an option. A discrete notebook that you can fit in your purse or bag can be the perfect option so that you can write the idea down and then expand on it later when you have the time to dedicate to writing it out.

I've worked with authors who tried to bring their laptops to their children's soccer games to fit in some writing. But the Wi-Fi was spotty, and then their computer died, so they sat and watched the game, trying to memorize the text running through their brain. A notebook will never have a dead battery. A notebook doesn't need Wi-Fi.

You certainly don't want the notebook's accessibility to infringe on your time, but it can be a real life-saver when an idea is just forming, and you need to get it down so that you don't forget it.

Inspiration Will Dry Up

Even with all of your amazing ideas and your dedicated time to write, there will be a day when you sit down and no words will come. You'll flip to your notebook and there will be nothing new. Don't panic. This happens from time to time. Often we get busy, and our brains have to go into overdrive managing work, and family, and holiday schedules, and vet appointments, and so on.

This can be a chance for you to relax and unwind, let your mind uncoil and give it space to think creatively. But I would recommend trying to use some of this time for other items related to your book. Can you start a mood board for your cover art concepts? Can you write one paragraph that will be your marketing text for the book? Can you begin to research podcasts that interview authors in your genre? Don't let this time go wasted. Being an author requires a lot of energy, and you can still make the most of your time by moving these other action items forward to help with your marketing down the line.

Before we move on to the next section, stop reading here.

Take out your calendar, planner, or scheduling app. Find the time in your schedule to write each week. Ideally, if you can write for an hour a day, that will help move the needle. But if you can only commit 30 minutes every other day, or two hours every weekend, that is fine. Start there. Block this time on your calendar for the next month to get into the habit of writing. Also, add to the shopping list to purchase a notebook next time you're at the store.

Chapter Two

Dedicate Space And Attention To Writing

I have met countless people who find out that I am an author and say, "Wow, I'm thinking of writing a book too." It is a fairly common life goal or bucket-list item. So, why don't they do it?

Usually when I connect with an aspiring author, I am eager to jump into questions about their planned book. What is it about? How much have they written so far? What questions do they have? How can I help?

More often than not, I get to hear about all the reasons why they can't write their book. They don't have the time. (Well, we just covered that in the last chapter.) Or they're going to write it once some other project is complete. Or they have kids. Or they have a dog. Or they have to get their oil changed. They list reasons for why they can't get the book written, but as far as I know many authors have children and pets. They tackle other life projects while they are working on their next book. So, what separates the dreamers from the doers?

More often than not, it is their focus or attention. You can set aside all the time you would need, but if you can't focus on the goal of completing the book, something else or someone else will make use of that time that you've allocated. Have no fear. There are ways to overcome this obstacle.

Now that you have been able to make the time to write and set some goals around how much you want to write each day or week, you will need to figure out where this writing will occur and find ways to stay focused.

Find Your Space

You should be able to write anywhere and everywhere. Some authors get very caught up in the idea that they need a specific desk and chair. The window must be facing north, and they need a mug of coffee that is precisely 93 degrees. All of these conditions are not necessary for you to be able to write. There are some writers out there who insist that they must be in their special space with everything just right. I would posit that they have not created a writing space, but rather a very elaborate procrastination technique.

Maybe you know that your mind will wander and that a snack will help to keep you focused. Maybe you can only write in the morning before the kids are up, so coffee will give you a boost of caffeine and help you put words into a sentence. But these factors should not become the conditions of your writing. When inspiration strikes, WRITE.

That said, as modern writers, we spend a lot of time staring at our laptops. To your friends and family, they may not be able to distinguish whether you are writing your book, rereading a passage that you are editing, or scrolling social media. Designating a specific location in your home as your writing nook will help you and those around you.

How this helps:

1. *When I sit in this chair, I am here to write.* I don't bring my phone and check social media every few seconds. I don't have a book with me that I have to finish reading. When I am here, I write. Having this set location can help you get into the right mindset to write.

2. *When others see me here, they know not to bother me.* I have prioritized writing and once I am no longer in that seat, I am free to chat or play.

If inspiration strikes while you are out running errands or eating lunch, use your notebook to jot down that idea right away. But use your dedicated time and space to enter those passages into your manuscript.

You know the space that is available to you. Maybe you need to take your laptop to the local library for an hour or so on the weekends to get the peace and quiet that you need. Does adding inspirational quotes in your designated space stimulate your writing? Would a sound machine with calming music help maintain your headspace? How about adding pictures of your family or from vacations? You'll find what works best for you. But, try not to be so specific about the exact location and position of the desk and chair that you are setting yourself up for failure. Any place where you can type on your laptop is a suitable place to write your book, but you may find that some locations are better than others. Once you have found the place where you prefer to write, make it clear to your friends and family that this is the place that you go to work on your book.

Dedicate Your Focus

I mentioned earlier that you will need to cut out any distractions, and it is worth reiterating. Just because you have made the time and found a space to write, doesn't mean you won't fall prey to shiny objects. Writing a book is work. As humans, we are programmed to maximize pleasure and minimize pain. (Work being the pain in this case.) This can make it hard to keep your focus on writing the book. Your adorable children asking you to play with them won't help. Seeing pictures of friends out at happy hour won't help.

It is okay to admit that you are human and will have periods of time where you are unfocused. But there are things that you can do to help maintain your attention on your manuscript. Even as I get ready to publish my thirteenth book, I still find that I need help staying focused. Here are the little things that I have done to help me stick to my goals.

Song Playlists

Creating music playlists has been one of my go-to techniques to help as I write my novels. Not only can I curate a list that allows me to get into the frame of mind of specific characters, but the music helps to drown out the other noises that might distract me. I also find that when I hear those songs during the course of my day, I start to get more ideas for the book. I also end up using these playlists when I am promoting the book later, and I share a link to them with my audience. These playlists are fun to create, but don't spend more than a few minutes on it. The point isn't to make something else to work on.

One key thing to note here, just because you are listening to a song that helps you craft a character does not mean that you can use that song in a book trailer or other promotion to sell it later without paying a licensing fee to the artist. The same goes for quoting those song lyrics in your book. There are a lot of hoops to jump through to get permission from the record company to use song lyrics in your book. I advise you to avoid them if possible.

Noise Canceling Headphones

Maybe music is too distracting for you. This is where some noise-canceling headphones can help. I have some days when I sit down to write that I just need absolute silence. Maybe I am stressed about other items going on. Perhaps I have a bit of a headache. No matter the reason, I find that if the playlist isn't helping that a good set of noise-canceling headphones can work wonders in terms of getting down to business and writing your novel.

Get Comfortable

This might just apply to me, but I often get chilly. Even in Florida, I am the weirdo who needs to put on a jacket or curl up with a blanket. When I write, I like to be comfortable. Otherwise, I get distracted, and then I get up from my writing space to put on some extra socks or grab a sweater, and before I know it, my writing time has flown by, and nothing got done.

Because I know this about myself, I prepare as best as possible before I start a writing session and have my comfy items nearby.

If you are always running a little warm, have a nice cold glass of water nearby or a small fan that you can direct on you to stay cool.

Another way that you can get comfortable prior to each writing session is to take a few moments to meditate. This can be as simple as setting a 5-minute timer on your phone or watch and sitting in silence, or using a meditation app that offers calm background sounds. During this time, clear your mind of all the distractions. The grocery list will still be there when your writing is done, the dishes will get washed, the report you have due at work will still be there waiting afterwards. Push all of that from your mind.

This may be easier said than done. One way I like to start a writing session when my mind has been pulled in so many different directions is to drop myself into the middle of the action. I either read when I just left off with or I picture the scene that I need to write that day. I pretend I have been dropped right into the book and try to focus on the finer details. Can I immerse myself in this situation? What would I hear or smell? What would I see? How would this make me feel? We'll go into other techniques for engaging all five senses with your writing in Chapter 7, for now focus on the scene that you need to write so that you can clear your mind, get comfortable, and settle into the writing session.

The point here is to understand the triggers that take your focus away from your manuscript and preempt them. Getting a warm blanket or doing a short meditation can be a simple way to help you dive right into writing.

Block Notifications On Your Phone

Speaking of triggers, if you know that having your phone nearby will be a distraction, then leave it in another room. If you are writing in a café, keep it in your bag. Or, you can try the facedown method that I mentioned in Chapter 1.

One thing I usually do is keep the ringer off of my phone. Most text messages can wait for a reply, and usually, the only phone calls I get are spam anyway. Having the ringer off makes it easier for me to stay focused.

I also turned off push notifications for most apps. I would find that the blinking light or the icon at the top of the screen would provide the perfect excuse to open up the app and check my notifications. Then thirty minutes and ten cat videos later, I would have no progress on my manuscript. Turning off notifications has been a massive help to stay focused when I am writing, and it has also helped me stay off of social media when I am trying to spend time with family. That's a win-win for me.

Turn Off The Internet

If all else has failed and you can't stay focused when you are writing your book, then you can turn off the internet to your computer. I know, it sounds crazy. But I'm not telling you to build a cabin off the grid thousands of miles from another human. I'm just saying that you should flip the little switch on the side of your laptop or click the button that disables your internet access. You can turn it back on as soon as your daily writing session is done.

I find that I can get more done when my laptop is in "airplane mode," and the easy access to the internet is shut off. If I absolutely need to check something, like a date or a reference, I can always turn the internet back on. But I know my weaknesses, and if I can remove the temptation to scroll, I find that my books get done a whole lot faster.

For every flight I was sent on across the country to work an event, I saw an excellent opportunity to sit with the Wi-Fi off my computer and pull up my Microsoft Word document to work on my book.

At this point, you should have set time on your schedule to write and methods for making the most of that time. And you should be comfortable writing when inspiration strikes and not forcing the words to come only when you are in a specific location. But how will you know what to write? That's where research comes into play.

Chapter Three

Do Your Research

E veryone knows that in order to write the best novel you must first immerse yourself in the world of your characters. Much like a method actor, you need to eschew your current life to really understand the setting and bring it to life.

NOT!

I've heard of famous writers going on ride-alongs with police officers to bring more reality to their procedural mysteries. But I suspect that the name and notoriety of the author led to that arrangement. Most first-time authors can do their research on the internet. In this specific instance of trying to bring authenticity to a detective mystery, there are countless podcast episodes given by retired officers turned novelists who provide clear dos and don'ts for authors.

And that goes for most research that you'll do for your book. First-hand experience or in-person interviews with experts are great. But you have everything you need at your fingertips nowadays. But how much research is too much research? When does it go from an effective part of your process to yet another procrastination tool? And what if it stifles your ideas when you learn that a planned plot point is actually impossible?

Maybe you decided to write fiction because you didn't want to confine yourself. You wanted to be able to write whatever came to mind and tap into your imagination. So, the idea of doing research may sound daunting. How can you let your creativity run free on the page when you have to do something as mundane and academic as research?

Well, research can be really enjoyable for writing fiction. That's because the majority of your study will consist of reading books! (If you want to write a book, the chances are that you enjoy reading books. If you don't like reading books, then this would be the time to ask yourself why you want to write one.)

Read Books In Your Genre

Before you can begin to dig into your book's plot, you should read books in that genre. And I don't just mean that you plan to write fiction, so you should read fiction. I mean that if you intend to write a Young Adult Romance set in space, that you should read other Young Adult Romances set in space. (They're out there, trust me!)

General research and a solid foundation of books that you have read over your lifetime will undoubtedly help. But as you start to think about what your story will be, dig into the other books in your niche. This can help you in several ways. For starters, you will understand common trends and tropes in the genre. The word "trope" has a negative connotation to some, but it can guide you. What are the rules of your genre? What will readers expect in terms of different dynamics? What can you bring to your novel that will differ from these expectations that readers may enjoy? You don't have to make an academic study of these other books and take diligent notes. But read them for their story, and you'll start to see trends emerge. Do you want to follow the trend or buck it?

When I started to write the first book in my time-travel series, I made a point to read as many books as I could about time travel and the multiverse. I wanted to see what was commonly accepted in the genre. Did I need to really dig in and define the multiverse, or would people who elected to pick up the book know about parallel universes and alternate realities? I also wanted to see what had been done before because I didn't necessarily want to create something that I thought was original and then find out someone else had done the same thing. This was incredibly helpful as I crafted my story. I continued to read books in the genre as I worked through my drafting process. You can do the same. You don't have to wait to start writing until the list of related books have been read.

Read Non-Fiction Books And Magazine Articles On Your Topic

While you will be writing a completely fabricated story, you will still need realistic elements to bring it to life for your reader. Think about the last time you read historical fiction. The author likely did extensive research on the fashion, technology, foods, and customs of that specific time-period to add authenticity to the story. Depending on where and when the book is set, the characters would have a particular manner of speaking and different underlying concerns about current events. His-torical textbooks can provide you with an incredible amount of context so that you can pepper in these details.

But what if you are writing about the future? Or, thinking of the ex-ample used in the previous section, what if your book is set in space? We don't know what the future will be like. And except for a few astronauts on the International Space Station, no one lives in space. Thankfully, there are a lot of brilliant people thinking about both scenarios. Scientists and inventors are always putting out articles on new potential technologies to improve human life in the future. Whether they are looking into sustainable energy, artificial intelligence, or enhanced technologies, there are many elements to consider. You can weave some of these into your story, whether it is an ancillary detail or a critical plot point. The same goes for life in space. What are the things that your characters will need to look out for? What food can they even eat? While you don't need a concrete answer for every possible question, it is important to do enough research by reading articles and books or listening to futurist lectures to build a realistic environment in your book.

For my series on time travel and the multiverse, I read several books by prominent quantum physicists. Thankfully, they were easy to digest and follow (probably why those books were published in the first place.) I made notes as I read and kept a log of terms to define and incorporate in my manuscript. This helped me to remain consistent in spelling and to check off what concepts I had clearly defined and what I hadn't. As I work on the next books in the series, I have notes on different items to research so that the next storyline is just as believable as the first.

Read Authors You Want To Emulate

You've likely been doing this type of research for years without even realizing it. Most writers can easily name their favorite authors. They eagerly wait for their next book release and devour each word. But have you ever stopped to examine what you like about their writing style? The chances are that what you like about those authors and their technique are elements that you may want to use in your books.

Again, this doesn't have to be a thorough study where you are filling pages of notes. (Unless that is how you process information.) This can be as simple as rereading your favorite book by an author and focusing on what details were explicitly stated and which ones your mind painted. You could also focus on the passages where you start to read faster because you have to know what happens next. Stop and reread that slowly. The author clearly built up the urgency there, so you may want to evaluate how they did that.

I've been able to focus on this with some of my favorite authors. For example, I have always enjoyed Stephen King's books. He is a prolific writer, but what I like the most is that his stories have a way of sticking in my brain long after I've finished reading them. As I went through and read *11/22/63*, his own book about time travel, I noticed that he repeated specific phrases throughout the book. This was very intentional and helped to carry the theme forward. I saw this in other books that I read of his as well. I tucked this bit of information away and have used it as I have crafted my own stories. The way he does this is very subtle, and that is what I have aimed for as well.

Another example of this is when I was reading *The Handmaid's Tale* by Margaret Atwood. When I first read this book, the TV series had not been created, so I didn't have any visuals to pull from except for what was in my mind as I read. I have been a long-time fan of Atwood's work, and as I read this book, I paused after she introduced a new scene or setting and closed my eyes. I looked at the scene in my mind and picked out the details that made it seem real and alive. Then I went back and reread the passage where she had provided some description of the setting. What she provided was a very sturdy framework for the scene, but not all of the details. I liked that she balanced just enough information to give my mind what it needed to work with. Some readers (and authors) love to review the minutiae of their settings. I like how Atwood sets up the framework for a scene, so I try to emulate that in my own books.

My last example relates to writing a series. This book is for first-time authors, so you may think that writing one book is hard enough, and you may not even be thinking about a series. Or maybe that is precisely what you want to do. This past year, I reread a series of books that I have loved since I was a child. The series is full of characters who had intricate backstories and histories. When I reread the series, I was looking for specific instances of when names were first mentioned. I discovered that a main character who didn't come into play until the third book was mentioned in the first chapter of the first book. I sat and thought about whether that was intentional or not. How would this author have kept track of those loose threads? Rereading the books from the perspective of an author who was writing a series gave me a new appreciation for the level of detail and organization that I would need to create in my own work.

None of this was hard work. All of it was quite fun and enjoyable. But the research was critical to my growth as a writer and the development of my story.

Before we move on to the next chapter, take a moment to search out some books that will help your research. You can save these on Goodreads or another online book service, or just make a list in a notebook. I have created a worksheet that you can access at AuthorYourAmbition.com/Novel for this purpose.

Chapter Four

Goals And Getting It Done

For the longest time, I was one of those aspiring authors who talked a big game. I was going to write an amazing novel, just wait and see. It would be a bestseller and my ticket out of a dead-end job at a toxic workplace.

But then I didn't write that book. I would get started, using the frustration that I felt from another pointless meeting or snarky email to fuel my writing. It was weak fuel and often I would leave the story only a few pages in.

This happened for two reasons. One, I was operating from the wrong energy source. My motivation was based on writing to escape, not writing to create.

Second, writing a bestseller is not a goal.

It isn't. It's a dream.

It wasn't until I had a goal in mind that the right idea and inspiration eventually found me. At the time, my goal was to write a novel in a year. Looking back now, I should have made it even more specific with a hard deadline on the calendar and a specific word count in mind for the first draft. But I was still new and learning.

The critical point here, is that my own books didn't get "done" until they were associated with a goal.

Set A Goal

Now that you have the desire to write a book, the time, space, and focus to make it happen, it is time to set your goals. (By all means, you can start writing at any time, but without a plan you won't get as far.)

I urge you to take this step for many reasons. The first is that a written goal is much more likely to happen than a silent wish. When you write something down and make it real, you feel the commitment more. Also, a wish is something that will *just happen one* day (like the prince rescuing the princess). **Novels don't just happen.** They are completed one sentence and one paragraph at a time.

A goal is something that you reach after taking specific, actionable steps. Think back to what first inspired you to write a book (or pick up this book). That initial inspiration will help you define and ultimately reach your goal. And it is crucial to keep your goal in mind. As you start to write and connect with other authors, you may hear about their plans to write a long series or launch a book a month or something else that may sound really daunting to you as a beginner. Remember that each novel is as unique as its creator. What works for someone else may not work for you. Keeping your goals in mind will help you stay the course.

Here are some elements to keep in mind when you write down your goal:

- Why do you want to write this book?

- Is your drive to write this book motivated by creative desire or financial gain?

- How many words will you have in your manuscript?

- When will you have your first draft finished by?

- When will you have the book published by?

- How many words will you write a day?

There are no right or wrong answers to any of these questions. Your reason for writing this novel is unique to you. And it is essential to know at the outset what the primary motivation is. If your motivation is to write a best-seller so you can make millions of dollars and quit your day job, the type of book you will write will be very different from if you just want to cross it off your bucket list, royalties be damned. You'll want to keep this in mind as you go through the entire process of writing, and publishing, the book.

The next set of questions relates to the book's length and backing into a timeline for reaching certain milestones. Generally speaking, novels are at least 70,000 words. Some genres tend to run longer than that, some MUCH longer. Once you know the genre, you can do some research on the standard that your readers will expect and set that as a benchmark. If your goal is 80,000 words and you finish the manuscript and feel that it is complete at 78,000, then you don't have to fill in 2,000 words of fluff. (In fact, please don't!) The genre word count averages are just that, averages. But this will help you to figure out how many words you want to write a day if you plan to complete the first draft in three months or six months.

Setting a rough timeline for completing the first draft is key. The hardest part of writing any novel is the actual writing. Having a date on the calendar that you are aiming for can help to keep you on track. If you miss it by a day or two, don't beat yourself up. Just focus on the progress.

To make this process easier for you, I've created a goal-setting worksheet that you can access at AuthorYourAmbition.com/Novel.

Self-Talk

This final step is the most critical, and even if you don't follow any of the other advice in this chapter, you must do this one thing:

Change your mindset from that of an aspiring author to an author, no qualifiers.

This can be the most challenging part because it is something you have to accomplish in your mind. But without this mindset shift, it won't be easy to dedicate your energy to writing and finishing your book.

From here on out, **you are an author**. You are writing a book. Not that you are going to write a book or that you are *trying* to write a book. These qualifiers open up the possibility that you won't reach your goal. Remove them from your vocabulary!

You have to start to think of yourself as an author and introduce yourself as such. This helps to reinforce the fact that you will meet this goal and gives you some accountability.

The world is full of aspiring authors. Everyone has a story that they want to share. The difference between those who finish their book and those who don't is all about their mindset.

Your task before moving on to the next chapter is to update your social media profiles. Next to your handle and location, add "Author" to your biography. Do it! Every time you connect with someone new, they will see that you are an author and may ask you about your book. (This also works for marketing the book when it is ready, but we're not there just yet.)

Whatever you have to do to signal to yourself and others that this is a serious endeavor, do that. But unless you start to think of yourself as an author and talk about yourself and your book that way, you won't be able to make it across the finish line.

And now, as an author, you may be thinking... but how do I actually write the novel? We'll start to dig into the mechanics in the next chapter.

Part 2: Elements Of Your Novel

Now that we have gone over the important factors that will make you successful, it's time to roll up our sleeves, flex our fingers, and start typing. While we have all grown up with them, we've heard them verbally, seen them in movies, and (of course) read them in books, many people don't stop to think about the mechanics of what makes a good story. As an author, you'll need to do that. While you don't want to analyze and over-structure the story to death, you can fine-tune a few key elements to make sure that your audience enjoys what you are detailing for them. Often when I meet aspiring authors who tell me that they are on their tenth rewrite before they send the draft out to beta readers, or they are taking a course on how to write dialogue so that they can pep up the novel they've been working on for years, I want to shake my head. Yes, learning and developing your craft is critical to your success as an author. But do you know what the most crucial element is? Finishing the book!

We all know the phrase, "you can't put a square peg into a round hole." But you also can't whittle that round peg until it becomes a toothpick either.

Please take the guidance and advice that follows as a starting point. If you feel stuck and unsure of where to start your manuscript, the information I provide in the following chapters can assist you. But, if you already have a strong voice, if you have a clear vision for where the story will go, if you have envisioned fully developed characters, please do not change everything so that it aligns with what I am saying here. In general, don't rewrite your entire manuscript based on any one book about craft or just one person's opinion.

The key to the success of your book is you. Sometimes you just have to trust your gut, and that can't come from anyone else.

Now, let's talk about nerdy writer things like plot and narrative structure.

Chapter Five

Voice And Structure - How To Actually Write The Dang Thing?

B y this point, you're probably thinking, *okay, okay, I get it. I need to be in the right mindset. But how do I write this thing?*

Writing your first novel goes beyond just getting your daily word count in, although that is a critical aspect of the process. You now need to build this story. You may write down the synopsis, a few sentences explaining what the story will be. But how will you tell it? Will we experience this series of events from the perspective of one specific character, or multiple characters? Will information be revealed to us in dialogue or interactions between certain characters?

It is important to consider the mechanics of the story before you begin to write. Some authors may get halfway through their story and decide that they need to change the point-of-view (POV) for the entire book. That rewrite may be time-consuming, but you may not know where the story will go when you get started. This is okay, not ideal, but okay.

In this chapter, I will review the choices that you will need to make as an author. You can make these decisions before you start writing, or you can change your mind mid-manuscript. There is no set rule here. Just know that the longer you wait to make a change, the more tedious your revision process will be and there is a heightened chance of inconsistencies.

This chapter, and this book, is by no means exhaustive. It would be impossible to discuss every technique employed by authors through the ages. What I aim to do with this chapter is to give you the tools that you will need to start assembling your novel. No two books are the same, and you will configure these elements in a unique way.

Let's start with the most important element:

What Is This Story About?

I'm guessing that most of you picked up this book because you have an idea for a novel, but need guidance on how to write it. Likely, you have some idea in mind for what this story will be. But maybe you aren't sure yet, and you are letting your ideas simmer.

I often think it is best to start with a one or two-sentence summary of the story. Maybe at this point, you have a full outline in your mind, go ahead and write a few paragraphs with that general summary. Or perhaps you know that this book is about a given character and the very unique event that happened in their day. Maybe you just have a character name in mind, and you're not sure how the story will unfold from there.

Whatever it is that you know about the book, write that down as your short summary. You can add to it as you start to piece together more of the story. These guiding lines will help you stay focused as you begin to write your novel.

Here is an example from my latest book:

The Alpha-Nina: Sequel to The Infinite-Infinite. Follow up with the crew to find out what happened immediately following Nina's return to Universe Alpha. What happened with the two Parkers? Did the team in Universe Delta continue their research? How did Marie and Femi figure out how to reproduce the same results in Universe Gamma?

You Need A Hook

One element I overlooked in my early writing days with a catchy hook. In fact, I usually wrote the book first, then figured out marketing later. As my author career has evolved, I realized I needed a better short hand for discussing my books with other authors, booksellers, or even crafting catchy short social media posts.

What I needed was a hook.

Sometimes this can be a catchy one-liner that gives the 'vibe' of the story. Other times it is a "this meets that" statement. This can be something you start with at the outset, or something you develop as you fine-tune the pitch for your book (whether you self-publish or query agents for a traditional deal.) The hook can also be your audacious 'what if' statement.

Here are some hook examples for my books:

The Infinite-Infinite: A feminist sci-fi take on *Dark Matter*.

Interview with a #Vanlifer: They're vanlifers. They're vampires. They're vanlife vampires.

Look at some of your favorite novels. They all have a great hook:

The Martian by Andy Weir: "Six days ago, astronaut Mark Watney became one of the first people to walk on Mars. Now, he's sure he'll be the first person to die there."

Book Lovers by Emily Henry: "One summer. Two rivals. A plot twist they didn't see coming..."

The hook should get a reader curious. It should get them to stop and read the full book description that you've carefully crafted.

To Outline Or Not?

The epic battle continues. Should you plan out every detail? Should you let the words flow freely and see where the story goes? Don't control the muse, but don't let her run loose either.

You may have already noticed a bit of a divide among authors. Some of us are planners. Some of us are more spontaneous. Some of us are a little bit of both. The terms used in our writing community are Plotter and Pantser. Plotter as in, you plan out the plot of the story before you begin writing. Pantser as in, you fly by the seat of your pants and just let the story unfold as you tell it (also known as a discovery writer). And then some identify somewhere between the two extremes of this spectrum.

You likely already have an idea of where you fall on this line. Reading the descriptions above likely triggered a reaction. Some authors can't think of getting started on their manuscript without a plan. Others feel that it is too constraining to outline. These are personal preferences.

For me, I used to start each story on the Pantser side of the scale. I began to write to see where things are going. *Will I even have enough storyline to make this into a novel?* Once I had about 10,000 to 20,000 words set in a document, I started to outline. I'm spending a lot of time with these characters, and I want to know it will go somewhere.

My process is a bit more organized now. I still have my document for all my thoughts and ideas, but I start with my pitch. Who is this book about, what is going to happen, what makes it an interesting story instead of just some things happening, what is at stake? Once I like the pitch, I outline from there what will happen in the book. I can refine my pitch and book description as better plot points evolve, but I focus more on the outline so I don't have to do time consuming rewrites. If I have the luxury of extra free time again, I may regress. Your process as an author may evolve and change as well.

Your book may be halfway done before you hit a point where you need a plan to fill in the missing pieces. Your book may never have an outline. Your book may have started as a twenty-page detailed chapter by chapter synopsis. There is no correct starting point for every author, but there is a correct starting place for you. You'll know what feels right.

If you think you are a Plotter and then find yourself getting frustrated because you can't think of what will happen in Chapter 17, give yourself a break and just write the first chapter. If you are letting the muse guide you as a Pantser and she is eerily quiet today, use that time to map out what you have already composed so that you can see the shape of your story arc.

There are pros and cons to both methods. If you plan too much to go in one direction, it can be tough to make a change when you think of a better way to introduce a particular character or drive a plot point. It can also be very tough to go back in and add structure to a lengthy document that wasn't going anywhere.

If you do opt to outline your book, remember that this outline is just for you. There is no one grading it. You can make it as detailed as you need it to be. This can be a bulleted list of the major plot points or a detailed synopsis of each chapter. Likely, you'll find something in between the two that works for you. As long as you have a method to keep track of what will happen in the book so that you don't have any plot holes or unresolved issues, you can outline in whatever way suits you.

But remember that the outline shouldn't become such a project that it distracts from actually writing the book. Some of the most detailed book outlines belong to the best procrastinators.

No one said writing a book would be easy. Every author deals with this challenge, so you are in good company. This is your first book, and you'll learn a lot about what works best for you, which will make your next book that much easier.

Determine Point-of-View (POV)

Once you have an idea of what you are going to write, you want to settle on how you will tell the story, and most importantly, WHO will tell the story. I am going to detail the most common points-of-view that authors employ when writing fiction. Like with outlining, you may not be sure of what point-of-view you want to use until you get a bit further into the manuscript. Again, that is fine. Many authors have found themselves meticulously changing tenses after they decide to rework the point-of-view for their novel. It is best when it can be avoided, but sometimes it just can't be.

You'll notice that second-person is missing from this chapter. This is for a good reason. There are a handful of examples where this has been done well. Most books do not employ it because it is so difficult: to write AND read.

Next, I will give you an idea of what each point-of-view does and how it can benefit your story. You will ultimately choose what works best for you and your novel. If you have lots of characters in a long multi-part fantasy series, you will probably find that sticking to just one point-of-view may be tricky. Or perhaps that is precisely what you are looking for. Your mystery may work best when the audience discovers the clues along with the detective, or maybe you'll also have the reader peer into the mind of the culprit. Like everything else in this chapter (and this book), there are no wrong answers.

First-Person

This is the most common point-of-view that we are all accustomed to speaking, thinking, and writing in. For that reason, many first-time authors start with the first-person narrative. In this point-of-view, the author assumes one character's identity and relays the story from that individual's perspective. You will use "I," "me," or "mine," statements to tell the audience what happened.

Because the story is told in the First-Person, the audience follows this main character through the novel and only knows what they know, only sees what this character sees, and so on. For a mystery, this can be helpful so that the big reveal can be kept a secret until the very end.

However, this can be a little limiting, especially if you have large secondary characters whose perspective will then have to be relayed in monologues or missives.

EXAMPLE:

"Jack, wait up!" I heard Sarah call from behind me. I just wanted to disappear, but I didn't want to be rude either. Had she even heard about today's fiasco? I couldn't even think about it.

I stopped short and waited for her to jog over to me, the sound of each footfall thumping against the concrete.

"What's up?" I asked, trying to be as nonchalant as I could.

An odd expression crossed her face, maybe she did know about my latest disaster. "Nothing, just wanted to catch up!" Her response was a little too cheery, maybe she figured she could distract me from my own tortured replay of events. Which was something I would have done if the roles were reversed.

We walked off towards the parking lot as I tried to carefully recount the parts of my day that weren't a complete nightmare.

Okay, I'm not trying to write the best story ever within this book, but you get the point. Jack, our main character is telling the story from his perspective. Because of this we have insight into his own inner thoughts and feelings, but we have to guess at what Sarah's motivations are. Is she trying to be a good friend or is she oblivious to Jack's dilemma?

Multiple First-Person Narrators

To answer for the potential limitations of the First-Person narrative, you can set up alternating chapters or sections where a different character is giving their perspective. With multiple first-person narrators, you can tell the story from numerous angles and switch to a new character as needed to keep the suspense going. This also helps if one of your characters meets their demise midway through the story; another character can pick it back up. If you have a large ensemble cast of characters or multiple plot lines, this can be an excellent option for your story.

If you select this method, you will still use the "I," "me," or "mine" statements throughout the text. This means that you will have to be very clear about who is narrating when the chapter or section changes. This can pull some readers out of the book if the transition is too jarring. You generally want to avoid anything that confuses or otherwise distracts a reader from the story. As you revise the text, you will be able to see if there are any awkward transitions. Your developmental editor or beta readers can give you feedback in this regard as well.

EXAMPLE:

"Jack, wait up!" I heard Sarah call from behind me. I just wanted to disappear, but I didn't want to be rude either. Had she even heard about today's fiasco? I couldn't even think about it.

I stopped short and waited for her to jog over to me, the sound of each footfall thumping against the concrete.

"What's up?" I asked, trying to be as nonchalant as I could.

An odd expression crossed her face, maybe she did know about my latest disaster. "Nothing, just wanted to catch up!" Her response was a little too cheery, maybe she figured she could distract me from my own tortured replay of events. Which was something I would have done if the roles were reversed.

We walked off towards the parking lot as I tried to carefully recount the parts of my day that weren't a complete nightmare.

—

I knew I should have left him alone, but Jack looked so despondent as he walked by. Even though I promised myself that I would leave him alone, that every time I tried to reach out I just got hurt, I couldn't stand to watch him shuffle away with that sad look on his face.

"So, how have you been? We haven't caught up in a while," I tried to play it cool. I didn't want him to know that I had been counting the days since he last texted me. I didn't want my puppy-dog crush to be so self-evident.

"Things have been fine, I guess," he muttered. I tried to not let my breath catch as he shook his hair out of his eyes.

All I wanted him to do was look over at me, to see me and say something like 'Sarah, you're too good to me, thank you for being there.' But it was too much to hope for.

Again, no one is winning any prizes with the above story example, but what I want you to see here is that we alternate between Jack's perspective and Sarah's. When this change is made, a line is used to delineate the change. We also learn more about Sarah's motives for reaching out and talking to Jack, who is clearly oblivious to her feelings for him. A best practice would be to shift perspectives at a chapter break and not mid-chapter. But if you need the POV to change mid-chapter, use the line break.

Third-Person Limited

Shifting our perspective to the Third-Person, we can also become the narrator who knows exactly what is going on. In this method, you will use "he," "she," "they," and "them." With Third-Person Limited, you will be the narrator who tells the story, but you will only be able to see into the mind of one character. While you can comment on what other characters are doing, because you are limiting the internal thoughts and feelings to one character, you leave some room for them to speculate and maybe guess wrong about the intentions of those around them.

A great benefit to this is the ability to drop in some foreshadowing or suspense. You can say things like, "little did they know..." because your character didn't know, but you as the narrator do. This is something that the same character would not "say" or "think" in the First-Person.

The limitation is that, well, this is a limited perspective. You are sticking with one main character and telling the story as they are experiencing it. You can narrate their thoughts and inner monologue. But you cannot do the same for your villain or romantic interest. You are still limiting the perspective, but you are doing so in a way that the reader feels less confined. While it can be easy for you to write in the First-Person, it can be jarring for the reader to delve into the mind of the character feet first.

The Third-Person perspective can make the reading experience more enjoyable and make the story easier to digest.

EXAMPLE:

"Jack, wait up!" he heard Sarah call from behind him. Jack just wanted to disappear, but he didn't want to be rude either. Had Sarah even heard about today's fiasco? He couldn't even think about it.

Jack stopped short and waited for her to jog over to him, the sound of each footfall thumping against the concrete.

"What's up?" he asked, trying to be as nonchalant as he could.

An odd expression crossed her face, maybe she did know about his latest disaster. "Nothing, just wanted to catch up!" Her response was a little too cheery to Jack. He figured that maybe she could distract him from his own tortured replay of events. Which was something Jack was doing when she interrupted him.

They walked off towards the parking lot as Jack tried to carefully recount the parts of his day that weren't a complete nightmare.

This is the same excerpt we read before, but the point-of-view has been changed. We learned all the same information and still closely track the inner-thoughts of Jack. We still can't know what Sarah is really thinking, we only have the context clues that Jack observes.

Third-Person Omniscient

Ah, here you become the all-seeing, all-powerful narrator. You know it all, what each character is doing and what they have done. You know their thoughts and motives. And as the narrator, you control how this information is metered out to the audience.

This gives you the freedom to switch the perspective from your main character to a secondary character as needed. Whichever point-of-view would be the most compelling for a given scene is available to you.

You still want to be very clear about whose perspective you are focused on, even as the third-person narrator. You can easily do this by saying, "So-and-so was doing XYZ" as you open the chapter. (Actually, that's not a great start to a chapter in terms of compelling writing, but by starting the chapter with the action this character is performing, you will clearly delineate who is the main focus.)

Another challenge can be to keep each chapter or section to one specific character. As the narrator, you are omniscient. But if you have only been providing the inner monologue for one particular character throughout the book and then the final chapter is a free-for-all of character feelings and thoughts, it can throw things off for the reader.

Dan Brown does this well in his Robert Langdon series of books. In each book, Robert Langdon is the main character, and we see most of the action from a Third-Person point-of-view that follows his train of thought. But Brown also weaves in chapters with secondary characters who are playing a part in the action.

EXAMPLE:

"Jack, wait up!" he heard Sarah call from behind him. Jack just wanted to disappear, but he didn't want to be rude either. Had Sarah even heard about today's fiasco? He couldn't even think about it.

Jack stopped short and waited for her to jog over to him, the sound of each footfall thumping against the concrete.

"What's up?" he asked, trying to be as nonchalant as he could.

An odd expression crossed her face, maybe she did know about his latest disaster. "Nothing, just wanted to catch up!" Her response was a little too cheery to Jack. He figured that maybe she could distract him from his own tortured replay of events. Which was something Jack was doing when she interrupted him.

They walked off towards the parking lot as Jack tried to carefully recount the parts of his day that weren't a complete nightmare.

—

Sarah knew she should have left him alone, but Jack looked so despondent as he walked by. Even though she promised herself that she would leave him alone, that every time she tried to reach out, she just got hurt, she couldn't stand to watch him shuffle away with that sad look on his face.

"So, how have you been? We haven't caught up in a while," Sarah tried to play it cool. She didn't want him to know that she had been counting the days since he last texted her. Sarah didn't want her puppy-dog crush to be so self-evident.

"Things have been fine, I guess," he muttered. Sarah felt her heart flutter. She tried to not let her breath catch as Jack shook his hair out of his eyes.

All she wanted him to do was look over at her, to see her and say something like 'Sarah, you're too good to me, thank you for being there.' But it was too much to hope for.

In this example we see both perspectives again to learn more about the thoughts of each character. To keep things clear for the audience the dash remains between the two perspectives. However, you could try to combine them to give a blended Third-Person Omniscient story, but this method can be more confusing for the reader.

<u>EXAMPLE:</u>

"Jack, wait up!" he heard Sarah call from behind him. Jack just wanted to disappear, but he didn't want to be rude either. Had Sarah even heard about today's fiasco? He couldn't even think about it. Sarah knew she should have left him alone, but Jack looked so despondent as he walked by. Even

though she promised herself that she would leave him alone, that every time she tried to reach out, she just got hurt, she couldn't stand to watch him shuffle away with that sad look on his face.

Jack stopped short and waited for her to jog over to him, the sound of each footfall thumping against the concrete.

"What's up?" he asked, trying to be as nonchalant as he could.

An odd expression crossed her face, maybe she did know about his latest disaster. "Nothing, just wanted to catch up!" Her response was a little too cheery to Jack. He figured that maybe she could distract him from his own tortured replay of events. Which was something Jack was doing when she interrupted him.

"So, how have you been? We haven't caught up in a while," Sarah tried to play it cool. She didn't want him to know that she had been counting the days since he last texted her. Sarah didn't want her puppy-dog crush to be so self-evident.

"Things have been fine, I guess," he muttered. Sarah felt her heart flutter. She tried to not let her breath catch as Jack shook his hair out of his eyes.

All she wanted him to do was look over at her, to see her and say something like 'Sarah, you're too good to me, thank you for being there.' But it was too much to hope for. They walked off towards the parking lot as Jack tried to carefully recount the parts of his day that weren't a complete nightmare.

Structure And Choices

Now that you have an idea of "who" will tell the story, you'll want to think about how it will be told. For those who are Pantsers and don't like to outline, this idea of planning out your narrative structure may feel constricting. You can start your draft and return to this later.

Still, before the book is published, you will need a clear arc to your story so that it is comprehensible to your audience. Sentence structure and word choice should be minded throughout the drafting process. However, if you are in a good flow state, you may find that you are cleaning that up during your revision process.

We'll first go into the narrative structure. Think of this as the foundation and frame of your home. This has the largest impact on the final outcome. If the foundation has cracks, the house will eventually crumble. The sentence structure and word choice are your design touches, the things that make the house look like a home.

Narrative Structure

As a life-long reader, I didn't always notice the narrative structure of the book I was reading. I just enjoyed the story. Once I began to write novels myself, I started to pay more attention to how the author was revealing the plot points. There are many defined narrative structures that you can identify in fiction. Below I outline four of the most common and effective. As you begin to write your story, you may start to think, "hmm, no, I want to reveal this information differently." With that, you will need to decide if you should change the entire narrative structure or employ another technique to get that information to fit within the frame you have selected.

There are other narrative structures that you may find as you do your research, this is in no way an exhaustive list. But these are the most common for a reason. Not because authors are lazy or uncreative. No, they understand that their readers need structure in order to follow the story.

Linear Structure – Chronological Order

Let's start at the very beginning with Linear Structure. In this type of story, the author reveals the plot in the order that things happened. By utilizing this style, the reader can follow what has happened throughout the story. There may not be a need to include dates or timestamps on your chapter headings, although if some time has passed between the end of one chapter or section and the beginning of the next, it may be a good idea to call that out. This structure is more straightforward for the reader to follow. However, you may have some backstory about your characters that you want to reveal. In that case, you can explain that through some internal monologue or flashback scenes that happen within a chapter or section. The point here is that the story follows a single and straight-forward timeline from start to finish.

A popular example of Linear Structure is *The Martian* by Andy Weir. The story follows the trials of marooned astronaut Mark Watney as he tries to survive alone on Mars. Each chapter continues the story from the previous one. While the character remarks on some memories from his time on Earth and traveling to Mars, the story's heart follows him through the many months that he is stranded on the red planet. The book ends with the rescue mission to take him home. There is one clear through-line from start to end.

Non-Linear Structure – Jump Around

The Non-Linear Structure is not necessarily the exact opposite of Linear. In this kind of novel, the author constructs the story in such a way that one chapter may take place in "the present," and the next may have taken place years earlier. This can be a tool to establish how characters got into a situation and their true motives. An example of this could be a novel about a bank heist. Perhaps the first chapter sets up the scene outside the bank, just before the robbery. The next chapter could take the reader back to when the person who planned the heist first met their accomplice.

This can be a very engaging way to draw the reader into the plot and keep the suspense going. You may end a chapter in the present with a bit of a cliffhanger and then take the audience back to a moment years earlier where they were in a similar situation to show the reader how the character may be conflicted about what is going on. The key to successfully executing this style is to clarify at the beginning of each chapter when and where the story is. This can be done with a timestamp under the chapter number or even a clause to start the new section. An example would be, "Five years earlier...."

A great example of this is *Vicious* by V.E. Schwab. The book starts with alternating chapters that show three characters in a graveyard in the middle of the night. That's odd. The next chapter goes back to when the two main characters, who are foils, met in college. With each grouping of chapters in the present and the past, we learn more about how these two best friends became sworn enemies. Until we reach the present day, and then the story continues from there. The pattern is established with specific dates and locations at the beginning of each chapter that help to clarify the time and setting for readers.

Circular Structure – End Back At The Beginning

This is a structure that is perhaps 99% Linear and 1% Non-Linear, depending on your page-count. In this novel, you would start at the dénouement of the story. (The peak of the rising action when the plot lines have come together and the big reveal/plot point is about to happen.) Then, as the author, you would spend the rest of the book telling the story of how the characters got to that place and time.

This can be a great way to capture the interest of the reader right away. You've just laid the scene for some stressful/impossible/calamitous scenario. Now the reader has to find out how they got there and what is going to happen next. (Note: we'll talk about establishing a strong first line or opening scene in Chapter 8, but the Circular Narrative Structure can be one way to begin your book and hook the reader effectively.)

There are several keys to success with this method. First, you will want that opening scene to be set apart as an introduction or stand-alone chapter. Then you will need to start the second chapter with precise details as to how far back you are going so that you can dive into the story. You will also want to ensure the first scene has enough clues or elements planted that when you bring them up throughout the story your reader thinks back to that initial chapter. This will help them to remember what the story is building towards.

Stephanie Meyer used this in each of her books in the *Twilight* series. The first section was a couple of paragraphs at most, but it set the tone for the rest of the book. Those who read the books before watching the movies would have been curious about the exact scenario being laid out. This created a feeling of suspense and danger right from the beginning.

Chuck Palahniuk also did this in his cult-classic, *Fight Club*. The narrator introduces the audience to the mayhem around him and wonders when he first heard the name, Tyler Durden. This introduction not only set the tone for the novel, but it also played a critical part in maintaining one of the biggest plot twists in modern literature.

Frame Narrative – Story Within A Story

The final example of narrative structure that I will review is the Frame Narrative.

The Frame Narrative is the story within a story. In this case, you could start the novel with one chapter where you set up the primary story and then dive into the full secondary story for the majority of the book until you come back out and wrap the primary story. You could also intersperse the secondary story within the primary story. As you may already notice, this structure is a bit more complicated. You have two totally distinct storylines to introduce and wrap up. And you have to make it clear to the reader which story they are reading as you transition from one chapter or section to the next.

Authors may elect to employ this structure because the secondary story reinforces the message of the first story. Or perhaps they want to further remove themselves from the primary narrative. Having the characters in the primary story narrate the secondary story allows the author to have an imperfect narrator. The character in the primary story may forget some of the finer details of the secondary story. Still, they are trying to convey a message to their audience, another character in the primary story. If it sounds complex, that's because it is. But you've likely enjoyed a book or movie set up in this structure.

One literary example of this is *The Blind Assassin* by Margaret At-wood. In this novel, we follow the life of an elderly author who is finally coming to terms with her past mistakes and her sister's death. As we follow her storyline, we read several chapters from the book that made her a literary success, The Blind Assassin. Through this, we learn more about what the main character did or did not do in her youth. This was very well done, but it was an intricate balance.

Some other popular examples are films that many millennials will be familiar with: *The Princess Bride* and *The Never-Ending Story*. Both are Frame Narratives, where there is a story within a story.

Most of my novels have followed a Linear Structure, although I have employed the use of flashbacks to give details on a character's frame of mind. I have used a Non-Linear Structure, too. Which was fun, but it required more work on my part to make it crystal clear to the audience what was going on. You may find that your story naturally unfolds and then look back and say, "Hey, this is a Linear Structure." Or you could find yourself with a finished first draft and think, "Well, the first half of the book was Linear, but then I switched to Non-Linear chapters for the second half." If that is the case, you may need to go back and review the way you have laid out the story to see if you can stick to one structure. This will make it easier for your reader to follow the narrative, enjoy the book, and, hopefully, leave a great review.

Sentence Structure

While your overall narrative structure should be clearly defined by the time you finish your manuscript, the opposite applies to the construc-tion of your sentences.

You should vary your sentence structure. Don't have too many short sentences in a row. A paragraph of simple sentences can be tedious. Your audience might think you are writing below their level. That would not be good.

Was that last paragraph a little awkward to read? Probably! Each of the sentences had a similar structure. But this paragraph has clauses. It has long sentences that provide a description, break up the monotony, and convey the message in a more engaging manner. And it has some short ones too.

You may miss this as you are drafting. That's fine. The sooner you catch this pattern if it exists, the better. You can edit your sentences as you go through and do your first revision. But you may overlook the extent of any repetitive sentence structure until you read the book aloud as part of your self-editing process.

If you are like me, you may find that you tend to have long, run-on sentences. I know this is one of my weaknesses as a writer. Whenever I go back to read my own work, I keep an eye out for any rambling sentences. Especially if I have multiple long, winding sentences in a row, I can break up a few of them into shorter sentences, removing excess clauses, and keep some of the long ones. This helps me to find a better balance in my sentence structure.

Don't stress out about this as you write. Let the story flow. Don't scrutinize every sentence to the extent that you don't get past the first paragraph. Get through the first draft and keep this tip in mind for your first self-edit.

Word Choice

The same advice goes for your word choice. Don't try to be perfect as you are drafting that it keeps you from finishing the story.

As with sentence structure, you should try to vary your word choice. There are certain words in the English language that you simply can't avoid using multiple times in a paragraph. *The, that, is, and, are.* All examples of the common words that you have to use.

But let's say that you are laying the scene for that bank heist we referenced earlier. You may find that you talked about the bank, the bank manager, the bank vault, and a banker in a given paragraph. Wow, that's a lot of the same word or root word in a short space. Not only will the reader notice the awkward, excessive usage of the word as they read the story in their mind, but it will sound silly if they listen to your novel on audiobook. In some cases, you could probably drop the word "bank" and just use manager and vault. You could give the bank a fictional name like AYA Savings & Loan. The audience will recognize that as the bank's name so you won't have to use it again.

The same goes for descriptive words. How many times can you say that one of your characters is beautiful? How about radiant, breathtaking, glamorous, picture-perfect?

What about the filler words for your dialogue? I've noticed in my own drafts when I have characters talking back and forth, and they each begin to speak using "So" or "Well." The characters are using the same no-value words that I try to cut out of my public speaking. I guess they inherited my bad habits.

If you think that you have been overusing a particular word, you can always search your document to check how many times it appears. For a book about trolls, you would expect that word to occur often. But if your novel is about a murder mystery and you describe one of the characters as "troll-like," you should only find that word once or twice in the manuscript.

I have collected my most common filler and unimaginative words. When I finish a draft, I comb through the document to eliminate as many of them as I can. You'll find this list of words to root out at AuthorYourAmbition.com/Novel.

Now that we have reviewed the more technical decisions you'll make regarding outlining, point-of-view, narrative structure, and varying your sentences and vocabulary; we can get into the challenging part: the craft of writing your book.

Chapter Six

Plot - Writing That Compels The Reader To Turn The Page

What makes a book "good"? What makes a reader turn a page when they are engrossed in a good story?

First, know that what each person likes will vary. Every reader has unique preferences. That means that not everyone will enjoy your book, no matter how perfectly you scrutinize each line. This also means that you are free to write the story you want to write and tell it in a way that you would find entertaining.

Because you've already started to think about the outline (or lack thereof) and point-of-view, you likely already have some thoughts on the plot and characters. In this chapter and the next, we will focus on these two critical elements of every book. If the plot doesn't keep moving along, you may lose your reader's attention. If your characters aren't believable or feel two-dimensional, your audience won't have a reason to root for (or against) them.

Plot-Driven Or Character-Driven?

In the last chapter, we looked at what your story would be about. You may have written down a one-sentence summary or maybe a paragraph. Because you know what the story is about, you may already know whether your book will be plot-driven or character-driven.

What does that even mean? Aren't all stories driven by their plot? Don't all characters have to move the story forward? In some instances, you may feel that your book has an even split between the two. But in each novel, there is usually one that wins out over the other. Either the plot points are happening to the characters and driving their actions, or the story focuses on characters and how they react to the unfolding events.

Let's continue with our example of a novel about a bank heist from the last chapter. In a plot-driven book, the chapters would detail each of the steps in the plan. The mole they planted on the inside. The codes that were purchased from a shady character. The tools and dynamite needed to get into the vault. Each of the participants in the heist would be acting out the steps to get to the end. But ultimately, it is the perfectly planned robbery that is the focus on the story, making it plot-driven.

On the flip side, perhaps the story is told with multiple points-of-view. Each chapter focuses on one character as they act out their part in the robbery. They ruminate on the actions they need to take, their conscience pulling at them to do the right thing. Maybe they are thinking about their family who needs the money. Will the getaway driver fulfill their part, or will they walk away? Will the bank manager make it home to see his children that evening? With each chapter as a short character study, it focuses on the humanity of each player that drives the story forward.

You will make this decision consciously or unconsciously based on your personal preferences for what you enjoy most in a story. Either way, you will need to make sure that you are dialed in on what drives the novel forward. A plot-driven story that suddenly cuts to a chapter with a detailed and emotional backstory on a specific character may seem a little jarring and out of place to the audience. Likewise, if you have been focusing on each character's personal angst and then go into a very technical chapter on the exact steps taken for the heist, it may seem like an odd interlude to the reader.

It is equally important to make sure that your book is not all plot either. Just saying what happens and providing cardboard characters with no emotion or personality is a recipe for disaster. As is a book that just gives the reader a view into the characters' minds, but nothing happens. You can't have a novel without both.

Plot

The plot of your novel may appear to you one day as a fully-formed idea. Or you may be inspired in bits and pieces. By the time you finish the first draft, it should be evident what the story's plot is. Ultimately, you want to be able to answer the following questions for yourself. These questions will be a guiding light to help remind you what will happen as the story unfolds, and then you can use these answers as you build your book description.

- What happens in this story?

- Why this story?

- Why this day?

- Why this character?

You'll notice that the first question is the only one that directly asks what the story will be. The rest require you to dig a bit deeper. Why should this story matter? In the case of a romance, why this love story? What's so special about it? Or in the case of a mystery, why this particular case and not any of the other crimes committed in that city or town?

As you go through this thought exercise, you may answer the final two questions about why this day and why this character. But if you haven't already done so, be sure you have this thought in mind. This isn't something you have to commit to paper, but it can help you in several ways. First, it will help you articulate why you are telling this story and spending your time writing it down. Second, it will help you when it comes time to describe the book to others. Third, it will help you define the point-of-view of your book.

We already discussed voice and structure in the last chapter, but many of these concepts can be defined simultaneously, or you may find that you get started and then go back and make some changes based on the answers to the above questions. There is no one perfect method for every author. But you should be able to articulate these answers. Let's say you are writing a dystopian novel set in the future. Well, you can pick any day in this distant future to start your story. And likely, you'll need to do some explaining about how the world got that way. So why did you pick that particular day to start your story? Is it a special day, or is this the first day of an adventure for your character?

Why this story? Why this day? Why this character?

I don't know Suzanne Collins personally, but many people are familiar with her *Hunger Games* series. The first book kicks off on the day of The

Reaping for the 74th Hunger Games. Of all the days that she could have picked in this troubling future, she had a particular reason for choosing this one. Not one day earlier or later. The same goes for her selection for the main character, Katniss Everdeen. Collins could have focused on any of the Tributes for the story. She could have picked the other winner for that year, Peeta Mellark. But she picked Katniss to be her main character because of her role in the revolution. (Sorry for the spoilers if you have been living under a rock and haven't read the books or seen the movies!)

If you are the type of author who just started writing and dove right into the book, answering these questions can help you to craft the first and second chapters to draw the audience in. The chances are that if you have answered for "why this day?" and "why this character?" you may already have your Inciting Incident defined.

If the term "Inciting Incident" is familiar to you, you may already know what I am about to detail. But many authors who sit down to write their first book may have never taken a formal writing class. And that is okay. That's why I'm writing this book to help you out. Some authors may disagree on whether there are actually more parts, but the basic features of every plot are as follows:

- Inciting Incident

- Rising Action

- Climax

- Resolution

Each author will want to carefully evaluate these elements as they are writing. Again, you don't have to have it all planned out before you sit down to write the first sentence, but these elements should start to come together as your story unfolds.

Inciting Incident

The definition may be self-evident, but this is the event that kicks off your whole story. Some authors may choose to start their story with this incident from the get-go. Bam! Page one. Others may set the scene and introduce at least one or two characters and the setting before this event. Only you can know what is best for your book. But you can't leave the audience hanging for too long. I would recommend not going further than Chapter 3 of your story before introducing this element. Otherwise, the reader may start to question why they are reading the story at all. Within the description of this incident, you'll want to explain why your character is involved. Maybe you already set this up in the exposition before this event. If not, you'll need to answer this for the audience.

For example, there was an explosion. Why does your character need to investigate whodunit?

Rising Action

This portion of the book is where your characters get going. The incident has occurred, and now they have to take action, they have to go on a journey, they have to work together, they have to solve the mystery. This is going to be the longest portion of your story. During the rising action, the clues are exposed, the journey has its twists and turns, and the character is challenged. This is the meat of the story. As the name implies, the stakes should get higher with each new chapter or scene. Throughout this section of your book, you want to be building towards the big reveal or challenge. You'll need to remind the audience of the stakes involved for your character(s) throughout the story in subtle ways. Remind them why they are on this quest, why don't they just say, "eh, this is kind of hard, I'll just have a sandwich instead."

Climax

This is it! The moment your story has been building towards. This is the battle royale that your character has been training for. This is when the detective in your novel reveals who committed the crime. This is the moment when your star-crossed lovers can finally be together. To define this moment, ask yourself, what is this story leading towards?

The Climax is usually towards the end of the book in the penultimate chapter. Depending on this moment, you may have several short chapters all at the end to bring the energy up as this final moment draws closer. If you know what this moment will be from the beginning, you can pepper in the right amount of foreshadowing and clues along the way. If not, you'll need to go back through the manuscript to add these elements in.

Resolution

The Resolution should be a relatively short section to close out the story. Now that the problem has been solved, the criminal brought to justice, the world set right, it is time to wrap up any loose ends. This is where you can give your characters their happily ever after. Or, you can plant the seeds for a sequel. It is typically the final chapter of your book.

Through these four sections of your book, you'll want to keep in mind the recurring themes. There is no set formula for how often you need to revisit these themes, but it should flow organically. The same goes for any larger message you are trying to inject into the story. It should be clear, but subtle. (Or maybe you don't want to be that subtle.)

Another critical aspect to consider in the early parts of your story is to determine what you need to define. Are you in a different universe where you need to introduce names of locations and species to the audience? Or maybe you are writing in this reality but, you need to explain some of the science or history that underpins your tale. You'll want to find an organic way to work this information into the story, so it reads like a novel and not a textbook.

After reading through this section, your head might be spinning with all the interconnecting details to keep track of. No one said writing this novel was going to be easy. Trying to break down the book into each of these elements makes it a bit harder, in my opinion. You have the story in your mind, start to write it out. You'll be able to look through your draft and catch these elements that you have already included and easily spot where you need to fill in some additional details.

Subplot

In life, there is never just one thing going on. The day that we have to make a huge presentation at work that will determine if we get a raise or not is also the same day that we need to pick up a cake for our mother-in-law's surprise birthday party. Oh, and a tropical storm is about to hit.

Novels work the same way. While you have just meticulously mapped out your book's plot, you may want to go back in and look at any secondary plot points. If you are writing a romance and you have planned out how the couple will meet, fall in love, break apart, and then come back together, you may already have a secondary storyline built in. What is the event that causes the couple to part ways? Were they vying for the same job? Did one of them choose family over their love interest?

Or how about a spy thriller. There would need to be layers of complexity to keep your main character from just strolling in and out of the secret compound. Are there other governments trying to steal the same information? Is there an old nemesis that is back to settle a score?

A subplot can be as simple as a blizzard set to hit, and the characters need to either get out of town or hunker down in place. Will they have enough fuel to keep the heat on? Will the pipes freeze? These elements add to the reality of the story you are creating and can serve as a device to push your characters to take the actions needed to move the primary plot along.

Some writers will find that this comes naturally. Others will take their time to develop these skills. For my own writing, my first two books had stories with a primary plot. It wasn't until the third book that I invested the time and energy into creating multiple subplots that would need to bring all the characters together right at the story's climax. As a writer, you will always be honing and refining your craft.

To help you define these elements of your plot and subplot, I have created planners that you can download for free at AuthorYourAmbit ion.com/Novel.

Pacing

Within the overall discussion of plot and subplot, the one phrase you should keep top of mind is pacing. How quickly is the story unfolding? Did you just have a very tense but short chapter packed with big reveals? Maybe the next chapter needs to be slower so that characters, and your audience, can process all this information.

Have you been leading the reader through a few more prolonged and detailed chapters? Maybe next, you need to bring it together into a quick chapter where you have a sudden twist.

The pace at which you reveal your plot points will determine whether your book is a "page-turner" or a dud. Here are some tips that you can pick and choose from to ensure that your story has a solid pace.

Length Of Chapters/Sections

There are no hard and fast rules to apply to how long your chapters should be. Some of the prolific American writers like James Patterson and Dan Brown have chapters that are five pages at a maximum. I find that there should be a balance of long and short chapters. When I provide details on setting or a character, I often have a long chapter because I have more exposition. When the action is really picking up, I tend to have shorter chapters. While I don't have a specific rule or pattern that I try to follow, I will look back through the chapters in my draft to see how many pages they are. If I see a big block that is pretty long (over twelve pages), I will go back through and see if I had extra fluff that I could reduce or any chapters that I could break up. I aim for a maximum of 2,000 words per chapter. In general, I know this will make the reading experience easier for my audience and keep the pace moving along.

Mini-Cliffhangers

One technique that I have seen many great authors use that I try to emulate is a cliffhanger at the end of each chapter or section. This will leave the reader needing to know what is going to happen next. I call these "mini-cliffhangers." While the entire book may end with a significant twist that will push the reader to pick up the next one in the series, these smaller twists or suspenseful moments will make them turn to the next chapter.

An example of this could be as simple as a character answering the phone, hearing what the person on the other line says, and responding with, "wait, are you serious?" That sets up a sense of unease at what is about to be revealed.

You could also end a chapter where you detail the point-of-view of your main character who is in a life-or-death situation. The scene ends when it looks like all hope may be lost. And then you pick up the next chapter from the point-of-view of a secondary character who manages to save them just in time.

There are many ways that you can build these into your novel. If this is a stretch for you, end each chapter as you naturally would and then add these elements when you go through and revise.

"Would I Turn The Page?"

It can feel daunting to try and incorporate each of these elements in your first book. But I have one question that helps me to focus and make sure my plot is solid. As I read through my own draft, I ask myself, "would I turn the page?"

It can be challenging to be objective when we are evaluating our own work. And most authors that I know tend to be more critical of their work than any of their readers. But, when you ask yourself this question, you give yourself the chance to review your work from the reader's perspective. You've read many books; you've probably started a few duds and just couldn't finish them. By asking yourself this one question, you are giving yourself a moment to critically pause and look at your own words.

Asking myself this question has often been the answer to any of my low-energy writing slumps. The words were on the page, the plot point was detailed, but something was off. When I asked if I would turn the page, and the answer was "no," I could review and rewrite as needed.

Next, we will look to the people that will populate our story: the vibrant cast of characters.

Chapter Seven

Creating Three-Dimensional Characters

F or many aspiring authors, the seed of their dream took root when they encountered their favorite character for the first time. Who was it for you? Who became your fictional best friend? Was it a book with a main character who reminded you of yourself? Or someone you wanted to be?

These enchanting characters have stuck with us for so many years. We still want to revisit them by rereading the book or watching the film or television adaptations. The people in these books feel too real ever to be considered made up. But they are.

Great writers can build memorable characters in their books with just a few very effective tools. They aren't sculpting these characters from marble. Instead, they use a few choice words here and there to create someone in your mind.

In this chapter, we will go over the important elements of writing three-dimensional characters that your readers will remember long after they finish your novel.

Character Descriptions

So many new authors start out writing their characters the same way. It's as though they witnessed a robbery, and they got a good look at the thief before they ran away. They provide gender, height, hair color, approximate weight, and details about what the person was wearing. This is an adequate description if you are providing a witness statement. *Not* for writing your book.

While you may write out this kind of description in your character notes, it isn't the way you want to introduce them in your book. This doesn't allow the reader to build anything in their mind. It also isn't very engaging. As an author, you want to leave room to weave in details about your characters.

I can't tell you how many times I've read books that within the first paragraph tell me flat-out: Maggie or Sam or whoever is five foot six, has long brown hair and blue eyes and loves coffee, but hates chocolate. *Oh well, thank you very much for blurting that out.* But the reader wants to experience this.

Perhaps Maggie is pulling her long brown hair up in a bun because she feels insecure in her classroom where all the other girls have sleek and well-quaffed blonde hair. Or maybe Sam is feeling insecure because he is five foot six, which isn't necessarily that short, but it's not tall enough for him to make the varsity basketball team.

A few chapters later, we could see Maggie growing in her confidence. She is learning to apply the right makeup to bring out the blue in her eyes and becoming more confident in expressing her opinions. No, she doesn't want to go out for a hot chocolate after the basketball game; she hates chocolate.

See how these same details can be presented without them reading like a laundry list? They don't necessarily have to be enumerated in such mundane ways.

And how about your secondary characters? Following this example, let's say Maggie has a crush on Sam. Likely, if Maggie were a real person, she would focus on one physical attribute that she finds the most attractive. Maybe it is his curly hair that always looks a little too long and shaggy. Or his smile, even though he has a small chip on his lower tooth.

Here is another example with these two potential characters. Let's say that Sam is trying out for the basketball team, and he is insecure about his own strength. He will probably notice which of the other athletes trying out have more sculpted arm muscles on display because he is hyper-aware of his own perceived inferiority. Sam doesn't have to describe every detail of the other people at try-outs. He can comment that they seemed like an army of super-tall and muscular professional athletes, whereas he looked like an amateur.

Each of these descriptions not only provides the reader with an image they can build in their own mind, but it also speaks to the frame of mind of the character whose point-of-view we are looking through.

Don't throw away your character descriptions by just listing out their physical attributes. Add context around these descriptions. Why was this character making a mental note of how tan and toned the other character was? Well, they were jealous that they just returned from a beach vacation that your character couldn't afford. Why was your main character describing the hands of their foe? Maybe they suspected that they got into a fight, and they were looking for potential bruises. Always make your character descriptions specific.

I still recommend keeping an ongoing list of the attributes you have ascribed to your characters on a separate document. You don't want to state that your character had chilling blue eyes and then later say that their piercing green eyes looked at someone. This document will become very helpful as you add more characters to your story. Not only to keep track of the details but to make sure you aren't overusing the same descriptions. It would be very unusual for everyone to be tall and thin with tan skin and blue eyes. That isn't real life. People are different heights, have different body types, and a whole array of skin tones and hair colors. Unless you are writing about a dystopian future where everyone is a robot that came off an assembly line, make sure to vary your characters.

I have created character sheets that you can download and use at AuthorYourAmbition.com/Novel.

Backstory

Who your characters are as people goes far beyond just how they look. They each came to the start of your story with their own life experiences. They were each shaped by the events that unfolded before. Whether it was a singular traumatic event, or an idyllic childhood free from worries, they are who they are because of what they have lived through.

While you don't have to detail their entire life's journey for the reader, nor should you, you as the author need to know who these people are. Is your main character generally a good person? Did they have any formative experiences that changed their worldview, or have they lived in a sheltered bubble? You need to know who they are when you begin your story so that they can develop as the plot goes on. No one person is ever static and unchanging. The events that transpire in your novel can and should have an impact on them as a person. Whether they fall in love, lose their faith (or find it), or make difficult life and death decisions, it will impact who they are.

Building this backstory can take time. One of my favorite exercises to do when I am stuck on writing my latest novel is to open up a blank document and start writing the back story for a side character. Not only does this help me to get to know them and think of more ways to incorporate them into the story, but it gets my creativity flowing as well. More often than not, the text doesn't make it into the manuscript, but the understanding that I gain about that character informs how I develop them throughout the story.

There are a lot of exercises that you can do to build your character. The internet has a limitless amount of writing prompts and I have several that you can access at AuthorYourAmbition.com/Novel. Here are some of my favorites to get you started:

- What is the character's astrological sign? (I sometimes switch this out for their Enneagram number)

- Write a letter from the character's point-of-view. Start with the line, "If you're reading this, then..."

- Where do they fit into their family? This is an exercise where you can go into some detail about their parents, siblings, cousins, etc. Or maybe this character never knew their family and had to make one of their own.

Each of these exercises is open-ended so that you can fill in the details and breathe life into your characters. You may never include their first concert experience or their childhood best friend's name in your book, but these exercises can help ensure that your characters feel real to your readers. You want your audience to connect with the people you are creating, taking the extra time to make them real and believable will always be worth it.

Believable Villains

In terms of believability, authors most often struggle with their "bad guy." There is a villain, a nemesis, a person who is behind the trouble that your main character is trying to fix in every story. This doesn't necessarily have to be a super-villain either. Maybe it is just someone that your character has never been able to get along with, who seems to always best them at everything they attempt.

The key to making this character believable is first to make sure you have an idea of their motivation. Why are they doing what they are doing? In some movies and stories, there are villains who just love to be evil. They get joy from being the bad guy. But in the real world, no one actually sees themselves as the villain in their own story. Everyone thinks they are the hero.

The believable villain in your story probably has a reason for what they are doing. They feel that they must protect the bank vault from thieves. They have been indoctrinated by the corporation they work for and don't see how they have been manipulated. They never felt respected when they were younger, and now, they have a chip on their shoulder and a need for power. You don't have to think that what your villain is doing is right, but you have to be able to understand what is motivating them.

This knowledge serves two distinct purposes. The first is that you can ensure that whatever they are doing to foil your hero is realistic and believable. If you don't know their motivation and just have them acting out against your protagonist for no good reason, the story eventually starts to feel a little spotty. No one wants to have a huge plot hole in the middle of their novel.

The second reason to know the driving factor for your villain is that you can spot their weakness. If they are carrying out a master plan to make their estranged dad proud, then perhaps the calming words of an older, wiser father-like figure will convince them to stop before it is too late. If they are acting out because they have been bullied their whole life, then maybe just a small act of kindness from your hero can quell the rage within just long enough to stop their evil plan.

Like your other characters, doing a backstory for your villains/anti-heroes can be very important. This will ensure that the reader will remember them long after the story ends. They may empathize with their pain and root against them, but you want the audience to have a strong connection to them nonetheless.

Take a moment to think of some of your favorite stories when you were growing up. Focus on the villain. What do you remember about them the most? Could you rewrite that story from the villain's perspective? How could you retell it so that the hero you remember is actually the one who is foiling their plans? Could you create a version of the same tale where the villain is justified in their actions? This can be a fun experiment to try on a favorite story first before applying this lens to your own creation.

Realistic Dialogue

Now that we have fully formed and well-developed characters, they will have to interact with one another. The most effective way to do this is through dialogue. Not only will you reveal important information related to the plot as the characters speak to each other, but you will also be able to give some insights into who they are.

While some authors find that dialogue is the easiest to write, others struggle with this portion of their fictional stories. Those who find it easy can sometimes err on the side of utilizing dialogue too much and forget to include some exposition to set up the scene. Here are some questions that you can answer to make sure you don't forget to add the description around your dialogue:

- Why are these characters speaking?

- What does each need to convey in this situation? What do they need to conceal?

- How are they positioned? Are they both standing? Is one sitting back relaxed, while another is tense? Are they on the phone or communicating via text or chat?

- What are the power dynamics at play between the characters? Can they easily chat, or is this a situation with an employee addressing a boss, a child addressing a respected family member, a commoner addressing a king?

- Based on where the characters are from and their level of education, does the dialogue match their regional slang and vocabulary? In this case, as an author who finds that writing dialogue comes easily, you may need to go back and add some context around what certain words mean.

- Is this bit of text necessary? Some authors will fill in every single word that two characters exchange. Starting with "hello, how are you?" and then, "I'm fine, how are you?" This can feel rigid and overly structured. Unless the person saying they are "fine" is clearly not fine and is trying to hide it, this is not compelling text. Cut the fluff and dive into the meat of the conversation. As an example, "After exchanging pleasantries, he jumped right in and asked the question..."

For the author who struggles to write any dialogue, here are some elements to consider to help you add this into the novel so that it is impactful:

- For any conversations that you have summarized, can you elaborate a bit more? You can quickly write a couple of sentences that Bobby told Rachel about the school dance drama. But, if you can build out the scene a bit more, you can provide some details about their relationship. Did Bobby just dive right in and start blabbing, or did he try to steer the conversation that direction? Is Rachel a hopeless gossip, so he knew to go to her to be able to spread the news and cause more trouble?

- I've often seen that authors who struggle with dialogue tend to have more stiff and unrealistic conversations laid out for their characters. Try to read through just your dialogue. Read it out loud and with voices. (You're an author now. If anyone thinks you are eccentric, it is to your advantage.) As you speak the words aloud, notice where the back-and-forth feels forced or stifled. Pay attention to your natural inflections. Do you start to speak more loudly and forcefully, or do you whisper? Add these attributes into the description around the spoken text so that your reader can experience this as well.

- There is no set rule for how often your characters should speak to one another. But if you are looking through your manuscript and see that you have avoided any dialogue for a few chapters, that could be a sign that you need to get them interacting again.

- Once you know the purpose behind what the dialogue will convey, you may still struggle to get going. In this case, write out the entire conversation from "hello" to "good-bye." While not all of this will make it into the final draft, it can get you started when you feel that you are blocked on this element.

Regardless of whether or not you find dialogue easy or difficult as a writer, there are some things that each author needs to consider when crafting realistic dialogue between their characters. First and foremost, there is a statement, and then there is a response. If one of the main characters just revealed that they are the mastermind behind the evil plan to destroy the world, the others' response should match that statement in magnitude. There should be gasps, shaking heads, muttered words of disbelief, and anger. You don't want to follow this up with a plain response.

Another vital element of compelling dialogue is to show the inner conversation that the characters are having with themselves. To just go back-and-forth between two people can be tedious. You're not writing a screenplay. You can tell us when one person is willfully hiding the truth. You can let us know when someone is very skeptical of what was just stated. Does a statement from one character trigger a memory for another? Tell us what else is going on.

One piece of advice that I discovered early in my writing career is often touted by many well-known authors: "said," is your enemy. If you have a dialogue going and you have every line formatted as: *"Text of the*

Dialogue," said so-and-so, your audience is going to get really bored, really fast. Did they say these words, or did they yell them, spit them out, mutter them? Use more descriptive words when writing your dialogue.

As we evaluated in Chapter 5, you'll also want to vary your sentence structure. You can start with one character talking, and then the line can be about how the next person reacts, and then they speak. Let's look at the examples below:

Example 1:

"I can't believe that Amy would betray us like that," said Tara.

"I know, she always seemed so nice," said Becky.

"What are we going to do now?" asked Tara.

Example 2:

"I can't believe that Amy would betray us like that," Tara shook her head with dismay, the words seemed foreign and unreal.

Becky nodded in agreement; she was stunned too. "I know, she always seemed so nice."

Tara knew they couldn't dwell on this information for too long, they needed a new plan. "What are we going to do now?" Tara locked eyes with Becky, hoping that her friend would know how to get out of this mess.

Which of those painted a better picture of what was going on? The second example included the same exact dialogue; the same words were used. However, we found out a bit more about how the characters were feeling. We also didn't have the same sentence structure and verbs over and over. The second example tied in multiple concepts from this Chapter as well as Chapter 5.

To help you improve your current dialogue or get this added to your existing manuscript, I have a list of verbs that you can utilize. While this is just a list of words that can replace "said," I often find that just thinking about the different ways that people express themselves gives me new ideas for what the dialogue can be about. *Hmm, which of my characters would proclaim something, and what would it be?* You can find this along with the other writing guides referenced in this book at AuthorYourAmbition.com/Novel.

Engage The Five Senses With Poise

Whether you are writing in the first- or third-person, you will need to tell the reader what the character(s) are experiencing. You'll notice that I haven't talked much about how to describe your setting up until this point. While the setting for a novel is a crucial element, I have it here in the chapter about characters.

Why?

Because your character has to interact with that setting, they have to be present to see the colors, smell the incense, hear the muffled footsteps, touch the velvet curtains, and taste the wine. Or whatever it is that your character(s) will do in your novel.

But instead of telling you to describe your setting or "set the scene," which are both very perfunctory instructions, I want you to engage the five senses:

- Sight

- Smell

- Sound

- Touch

- Taste

Instead of having your character walk into a setting, and rattling off the physical description, try to engage the senses first. Some genres specifically prefer more detail on settings. Others, you can get away with less. But regardless of the trends that you research for your novel, your character should have some sensory reaction.

Like with character descriptions, I would aim to avoid a detailed list that reads like a real estate listing. Unless we need to know that the room measures ten feet by ten feet because that detail will come back into play later, you can cut that out. Just like with the character descriptions, you don't need to list every detail right away. As an author, I like to start with sight. What is the first thing the character sees in this setting? Maybe the lighting is too bright, so they have to wince. Or perhaps it is dark, and the first thing that comes into focus is a map on a far wall. I'll start there and then move the character through the space to do what they need to in that scene. Along the way, I'll add in notes about what they may be hearing, elements they are touching, or if they smell anything.

I don't have a set rule as to the order of how the senses should be engaged. And in general, I try not to engage all five senses each time I introduce a new setting. Instead, I pick one that makes sense for that specific scene or character. Does your main character have an ear for language? Perhaps they often think about how things sound, but your villain who has perfect vision and a photographic memory often recalls sights in their sections of the novel. Or, if your setting is an indoor pool, it's likely the balmy air and smell of chlorine will be the most important details in painting the picture than a description of the rectangular pool with dark blue tiles.

Once you have picked out those key elements, be sure to highlight them appropriately. You can tell the reader that particular space (or another character) is stinky once. Don't add it to every sentence. If you say it well enough the first time, once is enough.

So now, you can add a beautiful array of well-described characters to your story. This cast will have depth and history because of their backstories. When they talk to each other and interact with their surroundings, they will convey so much more to your reader than just the basic details. With rich dialogue and captivating settings, your story will come to life.

At this point, your head may be spinning with all the different elements to keep in mind as you write. You don't have to master each item right away. Start writing to your strengths, and then you can go back in and add to any weak areas. In the next chapter, we will bring everything we have learned together so that you can write with confidence and finish that manuscript!

Chapter Eight

Bring It All Together

With so many different things to keep in mind as you write, you may think that it will be a miracle if you can get just one sentence down. You may think your creative flow will be interrupted with all these elements to check back on.

In reality, you'll write the story that is in your mind. Just like with anything in life, you'll know instinctively what your weaknesses are. After writing the first few chapters, you may find yourself in the middle of eating lunch, and suddenly you think of a new way to set up a twist. Or maybe you'll decide that you need to redo the entire dialogue from a specific chapter.

I wish I could tell you that there is a specific order in which you have to write the novel for it to be a success. But creativity just doesn't work that way, especially with the written word. You can edit, you can erase, you can cut and paste.

So how can you take all the advice you've just read and put it all together? Your answer will be as unique as you and your story idea.

Here is my process for bringing each of these elements together. Your approach may be completely different, and that is okay. Let's start to build this novel so that you can get your manuscript done!

Plotting And Planning

Throughout this book, I've referenced different worksheets and planners that you can use to help map out your research, plot points, and characters. Whether you use these planners or develop your own system, it is time to make sure that you have all of these documents in one place so that you can reference them.

As you use these guides to plan the big things that will happen in the book, you can start to outline the key elements in your word processer. (If you have already started to write by the seat of your pants, you can still add this structure once you get to a place where you need to fill in more of the story.)

If you use Microsoft Word or Google Docs, you can designate something as a Heading 1, 2, 3, or 4. When you do that, you can easily see the outline in your navigation pane. What I like about this feature is that when I decide that a particular chapter or scene needs to move to a different location in the book, instead of highlighting, dragging, cut, and pasting, I can just move that section in the navigation pane.

As discussed in Chapter 6, you'll also have more than just your primary plot in the novel. The best stories that you read will have multiple threads that all come together nicely at the end. Since this is your first book, you don't need to go crazy and have twelve subplots. That's insane.

But each subplot should have a purpose. Once you know the significant points of your main plot, then you can plan your subplots. One way that I keep these organized is by color-coding any of the details, dialogue, or even large sections of the outline. This helps me ensure that I am clear on which of the subplots I am focusing on for a given chapter. It also provides a nice visual to make sure I am not neglecting any storylines for too long. If I see too much of one color highlighted in the text, I can make a note to shift a few things around so that I don't leave the audience hanging for too many chapters before moving one of the subplots forward.

Example

Let's look at a story to put these elements together.

Short Synopsis

In this novel, the main plot is that Sam needs $1 million to save his family's farm; the bank will foreclose on it if he doesn't pay by the end of the month. After looking at all of his options, he decides that he has to rob the local bank. Sam doesn't want to do it, but there is no other way. Once he has made up his mind, he needs to enlist some friends to help.

Here we have the main plot. Let's say that we know that by the very end of the book that Sam is going to hit it big on the lottery, so we need to get him right up to the point of the robbery and then have him back down. Now in between him deciding to rob the bank and winning the lottery, he needs to recruit people to help with his task, plan the heist, and get to the bank on the day of the planned robbery.

Within this short bit of information, we already have several subplots that we can build off of. The first is that Sam has to have this lottery ticket, so maybe we need to establish at the outset that he has played the lotto every week, and he uses his sister's birthday. She died when he was younger, so her birthday is special to him. (Just with this one subplot we've added some backstory to our character; he is devoted to his family).

We can also have a subplot about a romance. Maybe Sam has a love interest that works at the bank, whether they are officially together or he just hopes for something more, this could give him an in at the bank to help plan the heist, or it could be a challenge if he decides that he wants to keep all of this from his love interest.

We also have the people he has to plan the heist with. They would have to have a big motivation to agree to help out. Maybe one of these accomplices is in some legal trouble, and he is the wild card. This character is desperate for the money too. We're not sure how this person will react to Sam backing down at the last minute.

Plot & Subplots

- Primary: Sam needs $1 million to save his family farm, decides to rob the local bank

- Subplot 1: Sam plays the lottery regularly (this will be how he decides to not rob the bank at the very end)

- Subplot 2: Sam has a love interest at the bank (unrequited)

- Subplot 3: Accomplice also needs the money; they aren't going to be happy about Sam backing out at the last minute

Now that we have our primary plot and a few subplots that we can play with, we need to build out this world that Sam lives in. We'll need to introduce and reveal a little bit about each character. First, we may want to convey to the reader what the character looks like. Sam could be of average height, average weight, average attractiveness. That's fine. But people want to read to escape a bit, so he should probably not be hideous. Keep in mind that not everyone can be movie-star attractive and tall. If you realize that you describe all of your characters as tall, it's time for some variety.

Let's say that our hero, Sam, has always been short; it has made him insecure in the past, so he feels like he needs to compensate by speaking loudly. Or maybe he has some kind of identifying mark. We know his sister passed away, which is why he plays the lottery using her birthday. *Hmm, could this be tied in here?* Maybe he was injured in a car accident, the same one his sister died in, so he has a long scar on his arm that he always tries to hide by wearing long sleeves, even when it is the middle of summer and really hot. This identifying mark can also be a liability in the bank heist plan.

Here is how we could add all of these details into one paragraph:

"Sam was thinking about how he could find money to save his family's farm. He had already lost his sister in a horrible car accident; he didn't want to lose the farm too. Sam was just your average guy with a big problem. He had chestnut hair and eyes, and even though no one ever saw it, he had a long scar running down his right arm."

Okay, not my best work, but you get the idea. And this certainly should NOT be the opening lines of the book, but it can be used as we establish who Sam is and what the inciting incident will be. Instead, we can break this up over several scenes. Early on, we could write about Sam commiserating to a friend that he will lose the farm to the bank. This friend could give him a hard time about playing the lottery every week instead of putting that money to the house. Sam could reveal that spending a couple of bucks on the lottery makes him feel close to his sister. The friend might feel empathy or compassion for Sam.

Later, we can have him interact with the love interest who works at the bank. Does this person look into Sam's chestnut-colored eyes? Do they blush when they see him run his fingers through his dark brown hair?

A few chapters later, we introduce his scar by having one of his accomplices give him grief about wearing long sleeves when they are all meeting in July in a place with no air conditioning. Sam could provide an excuse, but then we can reveal through some internal thoughts that he reflexively covers his forearm, not wanting anyone to see the scar.

See how we can break this out? It doesn't have to be a solid chapter of plot development and then a ten-page stretch of character building. It should flow together seamlessly. As the author, you will smooth out those awkward edges when you go through and review and revise the manuscript.

End With The Beginning

Revising? But you're still worried about how to get the story started!

Here is my best piece of advice. Even if you take nothing else from this book, I want you to keep this in mind: **You can, and likely will, rewrite the beginning of your novel**.

Many authors emphasize the opening line and chapter of their novel. And they should. This is the hook that will either grab the reader and pull them into the story, or they will put that book back down and move onto the next one.

When you sit down to write your first book, it can seem like a daunting task to write the perfect opening sentence. Many authors put so much pressure on themselves to execute that line flawlessly, that they never get to the second sentence. Don't let this be you.

Just get started, get going.

The great thing about working on your book is that you can continue to refine it. As you finish the first draft of your book, you will have a better idea of the overall themes, where the characters will go, and how the story ends. You may be able to craft that memorable first sentence better after composing the rest of the novel. The same goes for that initial chapter. Perhaps the first chapter you wrote will end up being the second chapter of the book because you write a new introductory chapter that perfectly sets up the narrative. Remember when we went over the different narrative structures in Chapter 5? Well, if you opted for a Circular Structure, then you will definitely need to add the first chapter later on once you know the finer details of the moment you'll be dropping the audience into.

If you go back to start revising your book (which we will talk about in the next chapter) and decide that you hate your opening paragraph, guess what? You can change it!

Refine Your Craft

If, after reading all of this, you think, "but I still need more help," that is okay. As authors, we all need more help, and we will all continue to learn and refine our craft until the day we stop writing.

The methods that I use may not work exactly for you and the story you want to tell. Or you may feel that your technique has already advanced past this phase. Maybe the way I've explained the components of crafting a novel didn't match how you learn best. Fortunately, I'm not the only one who can offer you advice.

I have found success with online courses. Perhaps this is because my first experience writing a novel originated from that college seminar. I find that taking an online course, like those offered through Masterclass, has been a great addition to my routine. Being able to take in one or two lessons at a time has helped me to think a little differently and challenge myself to new techniques each time I sit down to write.

In your case, you may elect to enroll in a writing seminar at a local college or try an online course. There are also many great podcasts out now (and surely more will pop up) that go over the craft of writing. You can listen to interviews with some of your favorite authors or discover new ones. These episodes can be inspiring on many levels and may help you pick up new ideas to refine your story-telling. One of my favorites for great author interviews on writing craft (as well as the business side) is The Creative Penn with Joanna Penn.

Another option could be to find a critique partner. This is another author who will review your work and provide feedback, similar to what you would receive in a creative writing seminar. The benefit here is that you don't have to report to class or worry about missed assignments. However, this partnership will also help you stay accountable to deliver a manuscript to review by a specific date.

The great thing about having so many options is that you can find the right avenue for you. You'll likely find that once you finish writing this first novel, you will write the next one that much easier, and the next, and the next. As you continue to produce more, you'll become more efficient as a writer. But you may also want to seek out more opportunities to learn and develop. Keep this in mind and don't be too critical of your first draft or from feedback from others.

And don't get so hung up on making the first chapter perfect that the rest of the book never gets written. Keep writing and revising!

Chapter Nine

The Revision Process Begins

After putting in the time and effort to work on your novel every day (or every week), you will eventually be done. If you feel like you are aimlessly rambling and the plot isn't going anywhere, take the time to plan and set a goal for when you will have the first draft complete.

With all the effort you've put in, the time will come when you get to write "THE END." Your manuscript is complete.

That's right, with every word you write, you are moving closer and closer to that finish line. And, since no one will be there for that moment, be sure to savor it. The story is done! Your first book is written. Crack open a cold beverage, dive into some brownies, do a happy dance.

And then the real fun begins... revising.

Just as you can stretch out the process of writing the first draft forever and ever because you are worried that the book isn't perfect enough yet, you can do the same with self-editing. I suggest that you try to avoid that. I've met too many authors who have been working on their first novel for years or even a decade. That's too long. That tells me that they are too in their own head about what is or isn't good enough. No book will ever be perfect, and no story is ideal for every reader.

Here are my tips on how you can have a successful self-edit to get you from the first to the second draft.

First Read Through

When I finish the first draft of a book, I feel like I can take a moment to breathe. The story has been told. It isn't pretty, and there are probably some unclear sections, but the meat of the story is down on paper. What a relief!

Before I dive back in and start reading it from page one, I take a mental break from the book. Some authors will type "THE END," hit "Save," and go back to page one and start reading again. That doesn't work for me. I usually need a few days or a week before I dive back in. This helps me in several ways. The first being that when I am excited to work on a story and finish the initial draft, I've usually pushed some other items on my to-do list aside. That break gives me a chance to catch up, so I have a clear desk for the second draft.

This time also allows any additional thoughts about the plot to bubble up. With almost every book I've written, there have been changes made between the first and second drafts that only came about because I gave myself some mental space. If I sit down and contemplate, "I need to think about if anything could be improved on my manuscript," I would likely turn up with nothing. And then I would find some memes of cute puppies online. But, when I focus my attention on everyday tasks like catching up on podcasts, working on other business elements, or cooking a meal, the creative thoughts pop up. I jot down the ideas that percolate and have them ready for when I sit down to that first read-through.

When I'm finally ready to read the manuscript again, I try to remove all distractions. I want to read the book as though I am any reader who happened to pick it up. The errors start to show themselves immediately. I'll clean up the grammar and typos that I spot, but what I am really looking at during this first self-edit is the story. I'll keep running notes on what needs to be included. When I get to that exact content a chapter or two later, I'll either mark it off the list or consider moving it.

My favorite method for reviewing in recent years has been the Microsoft Word Read Aloud function. I can change the speed to match my preferences, but the thing I love the most is I never miss a typo. (Or I find a lot more of them.) My mind may skip over missing articles or inverted words and put them in the right order. But the computer reading my book will not. This tool has highlighted many issues; it has been invaluable in my drafting and revising.

I try to get through the first reading within two weeks. (I do this in 30-minute increments because I know my deep focus lasts about that long; once I start to rush through, I know I'm not reading to edit anymore.)

This timeline can be a bit aggressive. Especially if it took you years to write the book. But I'm trying to go through the manuscript several times during the revision process. Just as you have a clear deadline for writing the book, set one for the first read-through as well.

Ideally, I'm looking to answer four primary questions during this first pass through:

- What could be more clear?

- What was left unresolved?

- What was repeated and can be removed?

- What was missed entirely?

After I have my notes on these questions, I can start to make a task list for the next read-through. Maybe I'll have to check that there is at least one passage outlining the background between this character and another. Or, I'll need to check that I didn't explain the same concept twice. I'll also have a good idea of what might be in there too often. With this checklist in hand, I'm ready to run back through the manuscript again. Each checklist that I create is unique to that book and the draft. I've never had the same one twice because each book is different. Your method for tracking your various edits and revisions will be unique as well.

Subsequent Self-Edits

By the time I get to my second self-edit, I am already starting to feel like the document looks more and more like a book. Then I see an obvious typo on the second page, and I remember that I still have a long way to go. As with the first read-through, I will clean up any obvious issues with spelling or punctuation. But I am always looking for the continuity issues and plot holes to fix at this stage. Looking at the list I made on the first self-edit helps me narrow down the items I should be addressing, but I am also adding new items to the bottom of that list to review in the next round.

Each book has been different for me and each time I review a book I am bringing my past experience with me. You'll start to pick up on which phrases you may have used more than once or which characters are introduced but never come back into the story later. I recommend getting two to three self-edits done on your novel before moving on to the next phase: the first outside reader.

Ready For Your First Reviewer

This is probably one of the scariest moments for a first-time author. The moment that your novel goes from "this thing I've been working on in solitude," to "hey, would you give this a look?" This means that your book is real. However, this step is critical.

At this point, you have written and revised the book yourself. The plot makes sense to you. The characters feel real to you. (After all, they live in your mind.) But when someone else reads the book, you get a new perspective on the story. You will hear from someone else what was still not clear, what was overdone, and what they wanted more of.

This first reader can and should be someone who is close to you. Someone who will complete the task of reading the book and give you honest feedback. This can be a parent, a spouse, a best friend. You'll work with editors and Beta Readers later. (You can read up on that process in Self-Publishing for the First-Time Author.) This first outside reviewer should know you and how you like to receive feedback. This review aims to get a gut-check. Did the person follow the story? Was the overall theme clear? Did the resolution make sense? Was there something that was a little too far-fetched or unbelievable? Or was that one juicy twist you planned apparent from the beginning?

The feedback you receive from this person can help you massage the plot further before engaging with a paid developmental editor or sending the book out to Beta Readers. To make the most of this feedback, make it clear when you ask the person to read the book what you are looking for from them. Set an exact deadline as well. "Can you read this by the end of the month and let me know if the story makes sense to you?"

While many of us writers will have a great experience with this first reader, some won't. If that person happens to only like science fiction and you just handed them a windswept romance set in Victorian England, you can bet that their response will be less than enthusiastic. Don't let that deter you. When you start to work with Beta Readers who like to read your genre, you'll get a better idea of how your target audience will receive the book. This first reader is just giving you the all clear on whether the plot has any holes in it.

Because you have already worked through your own list of revisions based on what you discovered on your first and second self-edits, you can pose questions to this first reader to see if you have adequately addressed these issues. Don't forget to solicit open-ended feedback as well. This first reader may spot items that you missed.

You will be able to apply their comments to your next draft and get the book ready for editing and, ultimately, publication.

Conclusion

That's it, folks. That's how you write a novel.

As avid readers and aspiring authors, we have spent years idolizing our favorite fiction writers. We may have even envisioned ourselves hunched over a typewriter, painstakingly punching out one perfect sentence at a time.

Those daydreams make for great television and movie drama. They may even inspire us to keep going. But the reality of writing a novel is far less glamorous.

No cinematic angles are capturing the moment of inspiration. There will be no whimsical background music playing as you type the very last word (unless you set your speakers and playlist before writing.)

Most of the aspiring authors that I have encountered are stuck at that stage: aspiring. They have a dream of penning a novel and the start of an idea. But they're waiting for permission to start writing. Or they are spending precious hours reading and rereading posts on writing craft. They're taking another seminar at a local college to help them refine their process before they get anything on paper. Sometimes they are getting sucked up in writer's forums and groups instead of actually writing.

There are an unlimited number of ways to procrastinate writing your novel. But no one else is going to write it for you.

I hope that with the advice I've provided you in this book that you are excited to get started. Don't be afraid that the words won't be perfect. I can promise you that they won't be even close. But, in the immortal words of Jodi Picoult: **"You can always edit a bad page. You can't edit a blank page."**

Get to writing, tell that story, and write your novel! I can't wait to hear from you when you finish your manuscript!

Acknowledgements

One of the most rewarding aspects of being an author is the ability to stop and reflect on all the people who helped me achieve my dream. Each book is a labor of love and while writing is a solitary exercise, editing and publishing a book require a team. Even self-published authors never "do it alone." There are always those helping out behind-the-scenes. Whether this team is helping with the technical elements of getting the book out or just offering moral support they are incredibly important.

For me, I have to start out thanking my husband, Jason. His incredible patience and support have been the driving force behind every book that I finish.

I also need to thank Debbie and Jeff who have been an amazing editing duo.

A big thank you to my mom for always encouraging me to read and write and showing me an entire world of books to explore.

Thank you to Cordelia Biddle, my professor from college who encouraged me to keep writing. My entire catalog of books would not exist if it hadn't been for her positive reinforcement.

Thank you to Jason and Teresa, my patrons on . Without that caffeine, this book would still be gathering dust on my hard drive.

Thank you to you, the reader, who inspired me to write this. I hope that you found this book helpful and I can't wait to read your novel one day!

Thank you so much for reading *How To Write Your First Novel - A Guide For Aspiring Fiction Authors*. I hope that you enjoyed reading it as much as I enjoyed writing it.

If you found this book helpful, please take a moment to leave a review. This helps other first-time authors find this book to help them on their journey.

To get more updates from M.K. Williams on how to write, self-publish, and market your book, head to AuthorYourAmbition.com and hit subscribe! You'll get a monthly newsletter chock full of helpful tips and timely author news.

www.ingramcontent.com/pod-product-compliance
Lightning Source LLC
Chambersburg PA
CBHW022102020426
42335CB00012B/799